# FAKE NEWS
# WITCH HUNTS
# & CONSPIRACY
# THEORIES

# FAKE NEWS WITCH HUNTS & CONSPIRACY THEORIES

## An Infodemiologist's Guide To The Truth

### PAULINE W. HOFFMANN

broad book press

Broad Book Press, Publisher
Cover and interior design by Andrew Welyczko, AbandonedWest Creative, Inc.

Paperback ISBN: 9781737517870
eBook ISBN: 9781737517887

Published in the United States by Broad Book Press, an imprint of Broad Book Group, Edwardsville, IL.

Library of Congress Control Number: 2024902911

# Contents

# Introduction

## The Game Is Afoot

**I THINK IT STARTED** with furries and the need for litter boxes in high schools. Or did it start with aliens and alien abductions? Perhaps it was Bill Gates putting microchips in the Covid-19 vaccine. Or the "stolen" US election. No matter the story, it all started with illiteracy.

Science illiteracy. Health illiteracy. Media illiteracy. Political illiteracy. "Fill-in-the-blank" illiteracy.

At least that was my initial impression. When the Covid-19 pandemic started, it seemed as though no one knew what was going on, nor what to believe. Theories hung in the air like the smog over Beijing. It quickly became clear that many people in the US and elsewhere had a limited knowledge of science and health and even less knowledge of media literacy. Misinformation and disinformation were rampant, and people couldn't decide fact from fiction. I assumed that people were just stupid.

I was wrong.

In believing that people were stupid, in a way, I fell victim to disinformation myself. The vast amount of disinformation that swirled around the Covid-19 pandemic was what is known as an infodemic, a pandemic of disinformation. In not recognizing the disinformation, and not fully understanding how widespread it was, I highlighted my own infodemic illiteracy. I prided myself on my many literacies. Science, health, and media are my fortes. I was aware that many people lacked several literacies, but I was not as aware of the depth and breadth of the problem until the pandemic hit.

I started Data Doyenne (a podcast and associated blog) in response to what I saw as an absence of science and rational thinking regarding the Covid-19 pandemic. I was bothered that people weren't taking the advice of experts but, instead, were seeking out their own "experts," who were not experts at all! The pandemic highlighted a general lack of science, math, media, and health literacy in people.

I also saw political, geographical, and cultural literacy problems. The infodemic had spread to include other areas as well. I expanded the podcast to include helpful information that seemed to be lacking. I invited expert guests to speak about cryptocurrency, the US filibuster tactics, and journalism, among other topics. The problem was too widespread for one person and one podcast. To be honest, at the time, I had no idea this problem had a name: infodemic. The term made so much sense to me—Information Pandemic. It described exactly what I was seeing, hearing, and feeling. Interacting with colleagues from around the world opened my eyes to this global problem. I was able to see what people were dealing with in many different countries and across many different cultures, religions, and politics.

Luckily, the World Health Organization (WHO) and the United States Centers for Disease Control and Prevention (CDC) partnered to teach medical professionals and communicators about the infodemic. They provide strategies and tactics that may be used to combat misinformation through their newly formed Infodemic Manager Training Program (I'm a proud graduate of Cohort Three!).

I jumped feet first into the infodemic cesspool. It is widespread and worldwide. One of my new goals is to help people understand what is real and what is not and how to think critically. Secondarily, I want to teach people how to communicate with those who may not believe the truth or who may not know how to distinguish truth from fiction.

I have the utmost respect for my infodemic management colleagues, but many of them are academics or are scientists, in one form or another. They do brilliant work in researching the infodemic and in developing interventions to determine the most effective "inoculations," against the infodemic. I wanted and want to do something more and different. Ditto my academic colleagues. Again, they do brilliant work, and their work adds to our body of knowledge in many fields. That said, many of them—some by their own admission—know how to communicate well with each other but not necessarily with a lay audience.

That's where I come in. I'm an anti-academic, academic. A scholar practitioner. A nerd who can distil some pretty heady information that we can all understand.

There was, and is, much being done to create and craft messages to counter disinformation, however, not as much to explain the infodemic itself—explaining science, health, and other topics to those unfamiliar with them. To be fair, it can be difficult to explain one's field or passion even though we are immersed in it and know it well. We aren't always aware of what others don't know. What seems obvious to us may not be to others.

Think about the experts you consult with and use. For example, you may go to your doctor, and she says, "I see you have a cephalalgia." A what now? Sometimes doctors forget that you didn't go to medical school and that you don't know all the medical terms. Sometimes they are just assholes.

By the way, cephalalgia? Headache. Which may have been caused by the doctor telling you that you had one.

## INFODEMIC AS PUBLIC HEALTH CRISIS

A study published in March 2022, by the Institute for Public Relations (sponsored by the Public Affairs Council and the University of Oregon School of Journalism and Communication)[1], noted that 60 percent of respondents think misinformation and disinformation are major world problems. Seventy-five percent of respondents feel that disinformation is a threat to democracy in the US. Sixty-three percent feel as though disinformation infringes on human rights. Disinformation makes people feel stressed and anxious, according to 52 percent of the respondents.

Who and what people trust is also interesting in the context of the infodemic. According to this same study, people trust families (35 percent), people like me (27 percent), and friends (22 percent). (As a note, "people like me" does not mean "people like Pauline Hoffmann." It means "people like ourselves and others.") The Edelman Trust Barometer Global Report[2], done each year since 2001, surveys more than 32,000 people from twenty-eight countries. Business is seen as most trusted, with trust in government and trust in media declining equivalently. More alarming, perhaps, is what polarization has done to our social fabric. Sixty-two percent say the social fabric has grown too weak in their country. What if you disagree with someone? Well, only 20 percent of respondents are willing to live in a neighborhood with those who disagree with them; 30 percent would help them if they were in need; and only 20 percent would want to work with them.

The infodemic is considered a public health crisis. A WHO bulletin[3] from September 2022, reviewed several academic studies about disinformation and misinformation and noted that, "Among YouTube videos about emerging infectious diseases, 20–30 percent were found to contain inaccurate or misleading information." YouTube is considered the second most visited search engine in the world after Google.

## MEET THE DATA DOYENNE

Before we start tackling mis- and disinformation, let me establish my street cred a bit more.

I have a background in science. My first degree—a BS—is in biology. I have a background in communication, both academically and professionally. My subsequent two degrees (MA and PhD) are in communication. I worked in public relations in health care for over a decade and currently work with our local health department as a senior New York State Health Fellow. I use my academic chops in the classroom at a small, private university in the Southern Tier of New York State, teaching undergraduates and graduates in the communication school. From me they learn research, conflict resolution, social media strategy, and public relations. And anything else I can teach them.

Or I think they do. I hope they do.

I grew up on forty acres in the middle of nowhere, east of Buffalo, New York. I found my love of science in the country, reading indoors, and exploring outdoors. *National Geographic* held an endless fascination for me and still does. The sharks and other sea creatures held a particular fascination. In fact, I was the nerd who had a scientist (shark expert Eugenie Clark) sign her copy of *National Geographic*. I still remember the title of the article Dr. Clark wrote and signed for me: "Sharks: Magnificent and Misunderstood."

Misunderstood . . . a bit of foreboding?

I also had an innate curiosity, which I think is required in life. I wanted to experiment and play and ask questions and get answers. I remember wondering how our utility bills varied over the course of the year. I asked my dad to give me the electric and gas bill totals each month and I plotted the expenses on a chart I had taped to my bedroom door. Before you think I'm too nerdy, I did have posters of the boy bands of the day on my bedroom walls like any "normal" kid (Duran Duran was a favorite—it was the 1980s after all). To be fair, anyone could have predicted how the utility bills would increase or decrease based on the seasons—we do have four distinct seasons in the northeast US, but I wanted evidence.

My father nurtured this curiosity. Come to think of it, he was probably thrilled I wouldn't end up a teenage statistic. Girls who post utility expense graphs on their bedroom door don't get many dates.

After college graduation, I ended up working in public relations/creative services in health care. I had no idea how much I would absolutely love it! It was here that I learned how to lead, strategize, and write for different audiences.

It was here I also saw science, health, and data in action. Health care is full of data—from admission statistics to emergency room wait times to readmission rates. I also worked on the first website for the health system, which should tell you how old I am. I learned about web analytics and how they should drive strategy and execution.

And I learned about conflict, working with difficult people, managing and communicating across different generations, working within a labor union environment, the importance of safety-in-numbers, and collaborating rather than conflicting.

Health care is comprised of different audiences across generations, genders, cultures, races, socioeconomic status—I could go on. I learned how to connect and communicate with a wide-ranging group of people. It's harder than it looks.

When I went back to school for my master's and doctoral degrees it was to study communication, particularly communication in conflict.

I became a professor, a job I maintain. I am a former dean, having worked in administration for nearly a decade. Even though I am a communication professor, I maintain ties to science. People often ask me about the connection between science and communication. Curiosity. Turns out science and communication (and other fields—we don't corner the market) require that you ask questions and dig for answers. They require that you don't accept things at face value. They require that you challenge the status quo. For example, I perform brain surgery as a professor (figuratively, not literally), and I've swum with sharks as a dean (figuratively, not literally, though that line was blurrier).

I still love sharks and now I swim with them both literally and figuratively.

At the start of the pandemic, I was increasingly bothered by the lack of quality information and the proliferation of untruths. I had to do something about it, so I started a podcast. I now write a LinkedIn newsletter titled *WTF? (What the Facts?)* in which I unpack disinformation and comment on current events as they relate to the infodemic. I also give talks about disinformation to anyone who will invite me.

For me, the next step in the infodemic evolution is this book. I am not writing for an academic crowd. They have their own journals and other outlets. Instead, we need to shift the narrative, identify truths and untruths, and teach people to do the same. We need to push infodemic literacy.

The data I presented earlier is just the tip of the infodemic iceberg. It's clear that information presented in a way that caters to a lay audience is needed if we are to truly combat the infodemic. It is not all doom and gloom, though. In addition to highlighting topics as noted above, I will share stories of those people/organizations getting it right. I will also work through several examples from different subject areas.

As your host on the infodemic roller coaster. I am glad you have chosen to take this ride with me. In the immortal words of Bette Davis in the movie *All About Eve*, "Fasten your seatbelts. It's going to be a bumpy night."

# What Is
# The Infodemic?

**INFODEMIC. WTF? WHAT IS THAT?** The term "infodemic" is relatively new. It was coined by journalist David Rothkopf in a *Washington Post* article from 2003, relating to the SARS epidemic, and is a combination of the words information and epidemic = infodemic. Do you remember the SARS epidemic? Likely not, since it didn't shut the world down the way the Covid-19 pandemic did. The World Health Organization (WHO) brought it into fashion, so to speak, during the Covid-19 pandemic, to describe the epidemic of disinformation surrounding Covid-19 itself, its origins, the vaccine, causes, symptoms, cures, etc.

The WHO considers the infodemic a public health crisis. From a public health perspective, disinformation is rampant. Disinformation is also found in a number of other areas and fields. One might say, like many zoonotic viruses (viruses that may be transmitted to humans from non-human vertebrates), it jumped from health to politics to just about anything you can argue about online. That's not entirely accurate, but it presents an interesting analogy.

What is disinformation? Does it differ from misinformation? Yes, in intent.

**Misinformation** is sharing false information without intent to harm. In fact, you likely don't know the information you are sharing may be false. **Disinformation**, on the other hand, is knowingly sharing information with the intent to harm and/or profit. Suppose I am feeling particularly evil, and I decide that I want to start a vicious rumor. I share this on my social media feed (warning: not true, not even a little bit): "Holy cripe! Did you see that Biden has declared war on Canada? Justin Trudeau stole his lunch money. #payback"

Suppose a student of mine sees my post. He is outraged that Canada behaved in such a way. He may also have a deep-seated grudge against Canada (they won't share their ketchup potato chips with us in the US, and they laugh at our attempt at poutine), so he shares the post, adding his own commentary. He knows my credentials. He knows that I am truthful—or at least he trusts that I am. That post then continues to get shared.

I just created a small disinformation campaign that could have deleterious consequences. I knowingly shared something blatantly false in the hope of starting trouble. My student, in sharing my post, shared misinformation. He didn't do it maliciously. He thought that a post coming from me would be accurate and truthful. No matter what you call it (misinformation or disinformation), such a post could cause havoc in many ways. This is a good example of why the WHO considers the infodemic to be a public health crisis.

Do we always need to delineate between disinformation and misinformation? Should we default to one over the other? I tend to use disinformation most of the time because I believe we are dealing with evildoers sharing false information to some end, whether it's to monetarily profit or seek revenge . . . or just be a jerk.

Throughout this book I will use the terms "infodemic" and "disinformation" rather than "misinformation." In my mind, this emphasizes how important and dangerous the infodemic is. The infodemic essentially weaponizes information. It preys on our fears and emotions to get us to act and behave in a certain way. It may be done for some gain, like money and/or power. I will also refer to those who create disinformation as "disinformationists." Let's get that word into the Oxford English Dictionary (OED) (#BigGoals).

I am now going to get a bit academic on you but in a fun way. I want to take us on a journey through the history of communication, and pepper that with a couple of theories. Don't worry. There won't be a test at the end.

## THE DISINFORMATION ORIGIN STORY

Disinformation is not new. In fact, one might argue that disinformation has been around as long as humans have walked the Earth. Allow me to provide a short history of "infodemics." Don't worry. I won't go back as far as Homo erectus but close.

How did people communicate before we had all the tools we have today? We can look to animals to answer part of that question. Animals communicate with sounds and gestures much as we do—our verbal and non-verbal communication. They also communicate using what they "wear." We certainly send a message with our clothing, hair styles, and makeup. Animals send signals with what they are "wearing." Think of the male peacock. When he displays his colorful feathers, it's like he's showing off his formal wear in an effort to signal to a female peacock that he's interested and she should take notice. Do we see deception in the animal kingdom? Ecological infodemics? Think about the animals who use mimicry for protection. The non-venomous king snake comes to mind. It has colors and stripes that mimic its much more dangerous cousin, the coral snake. One of my undergraduate college classes participated in a trip to Everglades National Park in Florida to study its ecology. Our professor was a herpetologist who, I believe, is the best person to guide you through the Everglades, considering the number of reptiles and amphibians in the park. He was walking us through some tall grass to get to another area of the swamp to look for ecological wonders, when he told us to look for the coral snake. He said it was called the three-step-snake. If it bites you, you have three steps and then you are dead. He then told us the king snake resembles the coral snake. If we see it, we are fine. Both snakes have black, red, and yellow bands but in a different order. I didn't remember which is which, and I didn't much care. If I saw a snake with black, red, and yellow, I avoided it.

Ah, disinformation! The king snake used this deception to make predators think it was the venomous coral snake. Success! Why? Survival. That's a pretty good reason to be deceptive, right?

Luckily or sadly, depending on your perspective, we saw neither. We did get a wonderful lesson in the flora, fauna, and hydrology of the park and avoided death by reptile. Success!

We humans may think that we invented communication and disinformation, but that is not correct. Watch where you step. That's good advice generally.

But, on to human communication. Aside from the verbal and non-verbal communication I referenced above, we also have other signals that have been used in the past to send messages. Smoke signals. Drumbeats. Horns. Whistles. Mirrors/glass to reflect the sun. Many of those techniques are still in use today. Several cultures still heavily rely on oral history.

Aside from verbal communication, we have written communication. In 3000 BC, papyrus was used for the first time. The first newspaper was "published" at the turn of the first century. Paper as we know it was first used about 100 years later. In about 1000 AD, we had the invention of pens, and monks everywhere heaved a collective sigh. They no longer had to etch things in stone.

Then came the invention of the printing press. Developed by Johannes Gutenberg in 1455, the printing press would revolutionize education and communication. Think about how learned men (and it was men) got information prior to the printing press. Any books were copied by monks, by hand, onto some sort of parchment—after pens were invented. Books and other written materials would have been available in a church, monastery, or other place where men met to talk about economics, politics, religion, and vaginas.

The printing press brought the written word to the masses and forced the monks to do something else with their time. This may be one of the first instances of technology taking jobs away from people. The elite men looked down on the invention at first. Of course, they believed that someone handwriting a text was preferable to something mass produced. How bourgeois it all seemed.

The printing press also made education assessable to the masses. With books came education and knowledge. If people beyond the elite cabal had knowledge, the power structure would be in danger of shifting like an iceberg at sea. The status quo was about to be upended.

The invention of the printing press is widely considered one of the most important inventions in human history. Why? Knowledge is power, and it gave power to the masses. It might be argued that it was the precursor to a free press because people were able to communicate with the masses on a scale not seen before. People could hold truth to power. Those in power were pissed.

## THE ROLE OF POWER

Let's talk about power. There are six different types of power, as detailed by John R. P. French and Bertram Raven in 1959.[4] You have legitimate power which is "given" to you or earned by you. For example, in an organization, the CEO has legitimate power. In a country, the president or prime minister (or other title for "leader") has legitimate power. It might be argued that the elite ruling class during the time of Gutenberg had legitimate power (as well as other types, but more on that later).

Expert power is shared by those who know something about something. They may or may not have legitimate power. Honestly, consider how often you have worked with those with legitimate power and wondered if they have any expert power, but I digress. I have expertise with the infodemic so that gives me a reason to write this book. I have expert power.

As a professor, I also have reward power. I can reward students for a job well done. I could also have reward power if I am able to provide something you want, like a raise or additional vacation time. As a proud dog owner, my reward power also extends to providing treats to my pups.

As a professor, I may also have coercive power. I can punish. I can give a student a bad grade (the student earns the bad grade—rarely if ever do people just give you an F if you haven't earned it). I can prevent someone from getting a raise at work. I can say to someone, "Hey, you want to get an A, guess what you have to do for me?" That would be bad and likely illegal depending on what the favor is. Where might I use coercive power? Ask my husband. "You want to spend the weekend with the guys? Mow the lawn first." (Don't tell him that a weekend away for him is also a weekend away for me.)

Referent power comes as a result of having relationships and building trust. An organizational leader has referent power if they treat everyone fairly and respectfully. They can get people to do things because of their reputation and past actions.

Those who have informational power hold sway over the information we need to do our jobs or live our lives. We might argue that disinformationists have some level of informational power. Wonderfully, so do those of us who are fighting disinformation.

It is possible for someone to have more than one type of power. If we consider the fifteenth century, we see who had legitimate power—the elite. They held all six types of power. With the invention of the printing press, they would have to cede at least informational power along with perhaps expert, reward, and coercive power. That's a great deal of power to give up.

Did Gutenberg have power? Well, it should be noted that he died penniless. One would think that developing such an innovation would ensure glory, money, and power for him. The problem? Sure, materials were more readily available, but no one could read. Literacy was a hallmark of the elite, not the masses. By the time that changed, Gutenberg was dead. That's not so different from today. I still must help some people upload photos to Facebook, so social media literacy is real for some. I'm not dead, so I have that going for me.

The printing press held sway for several hundred years, and then communication technology jumped into high gear. The typewriter (I remember pounding out homework assignments on my sturdy and reliable Smith Corona.), telegraph, telephone, radio, television, computer, internet, mobile phones, fax machines, pagers, email, text messages, smart phones, instant messaging, social media, video conferencing, artificial intelligence. Those are just a few of the communication technologies that have transformed how we learn, share, and communicate. The information we get from these technologies determines how we think and behave. The technology may change, but the end goal remains the same: power. And some wield that power for evil purposes.

## COMMUNICATION INVENTIONS

To dig further into how the evolution of technology affects media literacy, let's break down a few of these inventions.

---

**TIP**

Little known fact, the typewriter was initially created to help the blind to communicate. Look at us paying attention to the differently abled in the early 1800s.

---

What happens with the introduction of each new technology? People seem to go through a sort of "stages of grief" cycle. At first, it's "holy cow, this is fantastic." (Awe.) Then it's, "this is too good to be true." (Skepticism.) Followed by "Wait, will this cause cancer?" (Fear.) To "when in Rome," or "if you can't beat them, join them." (Acceptance/Adoption.)

---

### Diffusion of Innovations

Allow me to interject with a discussion of my favorite theory, in case you weren't completely convinced that I am a nerd. Diffusion of Innovations was first postulated by Everett Rogers in the mid-twentieth century. It explains how innovations, whether they be ideas (adopting a Meatless Monday), behaviors (weekly recycling), and products (cell phones) are adopted by people. One might argue that adopting Meatless Monday is an idea *and* a behavior, so there is overlap. There are stages associated with the theory. The first people to adopt are called innovators. Generally, they have the money and means to be first to use/do. Then you have *early* adopters. These folks watched the innovators and allowed them to work out the kinks. They are followed by the early majority and late majority. Pulling up the rear are the laggards who adopt last, if at all.

> When discussing Diffusion of Innovations, I like to point out that we want to look at the innovation and determine who our opinion leaders are. Generally, these are not the innovators but are the early adopters and perhaps the early majority. These are the people most of us look to in determining whether we want to adopt something. They may differ based on the innovation. For example, if I am interested in a new social media tool, I may look to a particular person in my network. That same person might not be who I would reach out to about buying an electric car.
>
> In the context of the infodemic, knowing who knows what and when, is important. Knowing whom people trust and why is important. Knowing how to reach people is critical. It's about finding your outlet and your ambassadors.

Back to our history of communication. The telegraph and telephone were going to revolutionize communication. Think about all the people we could speak with all over the place! I don't have to send a message via smoke signals or carrier pigeon. But wait, can people overhear my conversations? Will this end interpersonal interactions as we know it? Will I be duped by a prince from Nigeria asking for money?

Let's go back to some communication inventions as they appeared.

## Radio—Gah!

The radio may have been the first "mass" medium. It allowed broadcasts to be aired to many, many people in a large geographic area at one time. No other communication invention had that ability. It truly delivered messages to the masses. What were some of the arguments in favor of radio? It allowed a message to be delivered to so many at one time in a large geographic area. A con? Radio will spell the end of interpersonal communication. If we can just sit around a small box and listen to music or a message, will we ever want to talk to our friends or family again? How can we police this mechanism? What will it do to our young people? How do we make sure the truth is shared and not some lies? Do you remember "The War of the Worlds"? Sci-fi writer, H.G. Wells, wrote a fictionalized account of an alien attack. It was broadcast live on the radio and people who were listening thought it was real, even though there was a disclaimer at the start of the program noting that it was fiction. There was widespread panic and much SPAM consumed in bomb shelters that evening. The story was delivered in such a way that it appealed to people's fears. They either forgot or didn't hear the disclaimer.

It's probably just a fad.

## Television – the "Boob Tube"

What were some of the arguments in favor of television? It allows a message to be delivered to so many around the world at the same time. A con? Television will spell the end of interpersonal communication (because radio didn't do that, so this one must). If we can just sit around a small box and watch the news or a program, will we ever want to talk to our friends or family again? How can we police this mechanism? How do we make sure the truth is shared? What will it do to our young people?

It's probably just a fad.

## The Computer: You'll Get Carpal Tunnel

What were some of the arguments in favor of computers? It allows us to work more efficiently and effectively—once people got over the learning curve. A con? Computers will spell the end of interpersonal communication (because radio and television didn't do that, so this one must). If we can just sit around a small box and type, will we ever want to talk to our friends or family again? How can we police this mechanism? How do we make sure the truth is shared? What will it do to our young people?

It's probably just a fad.

## The Internet, Cell Phones, Social Media, and Everything After

What were some of the arguments in favor of cell phones, internet, and social media? They allow us unprecedented access to all the knowledge of the world! And fast. A con? Cell phones, the internet, and social media will spell the end of interpersonal communication, for real this time! If we can just sit around a small box (interesting that everything seems to be a small box or box-like item) and watch the news or a program, will we ever want to talk to our friends or family again? How can we police this mechanism? How do we make sure the truth is shared? What will it do to our young people?

It's probably just a fad.

You are probably sick of seeing the same paragraph over and over with some different words but are you noticing a pattern?

I have bad news if you are anti-communication technology. We still have radios, television, computers, cell phones, the internet, and social media. We like our boxes. We still have family and friends, and we talk to them. Young people grow and mature (many of them) and produce more young people who survive new communication technologies and grow and mature (some of them). We're good.

But what about Artificial Intelligence (AI)? Did I just make your head explode? Guess what we are saying about AI? (I think you can take the leap with me and see where I am going with this.) Additionally, AI is going to be taking jobs away from people in way that the other technologies didn't. If AI can "think" for us, then what will we do? In this vein, AI may be compared with other mass market inventions like the assembly line or the computer. Those inventions were intended to modernize industry and streamline production—whether it be production of physical products or ideas. That did happen, but it also opened the door to other industries and jobs. Someone must work on the assembly lines and program the computers. Whatever happened to the transcribing monks? They found other occupations.

What happened with each new communication technology? People thought they would lose their jobs. Some jobs diminish or go away altogether, but other jobs get created. I don't think any leaders of countries killed those who created these new technologies because, while there may be evil ways to use them, there are also many benefits. Does it streamline our communication? Does it free up time so that we may do other things? Does it help us to build community? Does it help educate us?

Along with that, we may say that with each new technology come evildoers ready to exploit it for their own gain. Because of the history of communication and its repetitive nature, I am a huge proponent of figuring out how to use these tools for good, and understanding the bad. I do not advocate abstinence. It doesn't work.

We have seen how communication technologies have evolved and been adopted over the centuries. We can all likely recount stories of how communication technologies have helped us and hindered us. I mentioned my Smith Corona typewriter. I don't use it anymore, but I sure did like it. I am typing this book on a laptop. I am getting information via the internet (and other places, but the internet primarily). I am posting updates and information on social media. I am using my cell phone to do pretty much everything.

None of what I've noted is a fad. When in Rome, evolve and adapt.

How do I know if the information I am accessing on the internet is accurate? This book is about the infodemic. What if I'm wrong? What is out there? Where did it come from?

Another con you will hear associated with communication technologies is the speed with which information may be shared. Also, the type of information which may be shared. I could lie all day long online and that's perfectly okay. I can share and do anything (within reason). What's to stop me? Guess what? I could have done that with the other inventions. People have lied since people could communicate. It's not new. Even nature lies as we saw with our Everglades king snakes.

This is where disinformation really takes off. The age of social media and a 24/7 news cycle makes it incredibly difficult to report the news, let alone try to debunk myths that are out there.

## THE ROLE OF COMMUNICATION

Before we get too much further along, let me describe communication. **Figure 1** (see next page) shows a common communication map. What do each of the pieces mean?

In any communication scenario, you have someone who is the sender. In the case of this book, I am the sender of information. I have a message that I need to share with you, and I craft that message in a way that is easily understood—or in a way I believe is easily understood. I encode that message for you, which just means that I am putting words to paper or thoughts together. The channel carries that message to you, the receiver, who decodes that message for themselves. The channel in this case is the

**FIGURE 1:** Communications Map

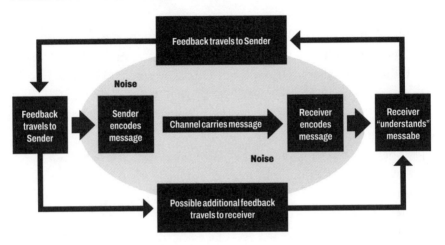

book. It could also be my LinkedIn newsletter. It could be social media. It could be a workshop I'm conducting in which you are a participant. You receive the message and indicate to me that you understand it. You may do that by sharing the book with your friends (though I hope you won't and that you will encourage them to buy it because I have dogs to feed). You may reply to my post on LinkedIn or other social media. You may nod your head in my workshop. You may also provide feedback nonverbally. If we are in person, I may see a quizzical look on your face. Or I may see you sleeping. Both would indicate to me that you didn't get the message. All those things are "feedback to the sender." I then re-encode the message because I really, really want you to get it.

I'm describing two-way communication, which is ideal. Not all communication channels allow for two-way communication. Not all senders want two-way communication. If I am creating a disinformation campaign, I likely want you to indicate whether you got the message. That could be by looking at the analytics associated with social media posts. It could be the number of "mainstream" media stories about the disinformation. I would argue I want the same for any communication campaign. I want to know I was successful in my communication.

You may have noticed "noise" in the diagram. What is noise? Noise could be literal noise like static on a phone line, an unstable internet connection on a Zoom call, kids screaming, or dogs barking in the background of the same Zoom call. It could also be any other distraction. If you see me in person and you don't like the earrings I am wearing, that might be all you are focused on. What if you had a fight with your significant other that morning? That might be dominating your thoughts and preventing you from getting and understanding my message. What if I am the speaker just before lunch and you are hungry? What if I was speaking in French? I would be impressed with myself because I don't speak French. You might not understand the language I am using or may not be able to cut through my heavy accent. Or if I am a scientist who doesn't realize that I am speaking in my profession's jargon, you may have no idea what I am saying and no way of asking me to clarify.

What do you do if you are faced with noise? Some of you may try to cut through the clutter. I suspect most of you will find someone else who can answer your question. And that person may not be qualified but has figured out the art of communication. And that provides an opening for disinformation.

## THE ROLE OF DISINFORMATION

Before we get too ahead of ourselves, let's look at some examples of disinformation through the ages. I won't go back as far as the printing press, but I could (Chinese or German).

I've mentioned that disinformation is not new. You may have heard it called "propaganda." Are the two the same? I would argue, yes. When you read the word "propaganda" what did you think of? Some may have thought of public relations (and that makes me sad since I work in and teach public relations). Some may have thought of political advertising campaigns or advertising campaigns in general. Some may have thought of wartime messaging. "Fake news?" Something else?

I like to use political examples because there are so many of them. Disinformation in politics is as old as, well, politics. Every year we see advertising campaigns for those seeking elected office. Many of those campaigns are either borderline or outright disinformation. They work! Why? The same reason they work in other areas: They play on our fears.

They reinforce our already held beliefs. They allow us to find our people and others like us. What are some examples? I could use current examples—they are everywhere—but let's look to history.

Kerwin Swint, professor of political science at Kennesaw State University and the author of *Mudslingers: The Top 25 Dirtiest Political Campaigns of All Time*,[5] notes that disinformation or negative campaigning in US politics is hardly new. We like to think of our founding fathers as righteous. They are no different from current politicians, except with more florid descriptions and funkier pens. A war of words between John Adams and Thomas Jefferson in the presidential election of 1800 is one example.

Jefferson said that Adams was a "hideous hermaphroditical character, which has neither the force and firmness of a man, nor the gentleness and sensibility of a woman." To translate to twenty-first century parlance, Jefferson thought Adams was a coward. Adams retorted by saying something similar in terms of character assassination.

The election swung in Jefferson's favor when he said that Adams wanted to go to war with France, an outright lie he knew would help him win because the US was quite tired of war in 1800. Again, preying on our fears. We were tired of war. No more war. No one thought to check to see if Jefferson's assertion was true. Google didn't exist in 1800. Fact-checking was time consuming and difficult—not unlike today even though we have Google.

Let's look to another historical example that has reverberations yet today—vaccines. Ever since vaccines were discovered and used, there has been propaganda about them. The first known vaccine was the smallpox vaccine. It is commonly attributed to use during the American Revolutionary War, though there is evidence of using a similar inoculation method in China in the ninth century.[6] The ninth century! And China! Do we also need historical literacy or what? When the vaccine became more widely available, we saw the first anti-vaccine movement. What would happen if you got the smallpox vaccine? Because it was made using the similar cowpox virus, anti-vaccine campaigns showed images of people growing cow heads. Needless to say, no one grew a cow head, but the concept played to our fears. It was bad enough that people wore powdered wigs and corsets made of whale bone.

"No one wants to grow a cow head, so why take the chance?" Notice the redirection of the argument. The vaccine is intended to save lives. If you know anything about smallpox, you know it is highly contagious, often fatal, always miserable. The vaccine can prevent all of that, but the message is—cow head. Truthfully, I'd rather grow a cow head than get smallpox.

If you look at many remedies, cures, or helpful medicines, when they appeared, there was a similar backlash. Fluoride is so common in our drinking water that we don't even think about it anymore. That is, until it isn't in the water. A case in Buffalo, New York, noted that fluoride had been removed from the drinking water and has been absent for seven years.[7] Residents were not informed of this change. Residents found out when the incidence of tooth decay increased for no apparent reason. When fluoride was first introduced, there was a disinformation campaign deriding it and noting that it would ruin your teeth. Again, not true.

Then we have quack medicine and charlatans hawking snake oil. As an aside, the term "snake oil salesman" came about because of appropriation and shoddy medicine. The Chinese brought snake oil liniments with then from China when they came to live and work in the United States in the nineteenth century. Their products worked to relieve aches and pains. Some savvy and dishonest folks made less effective, and sometimes outright worthless, products and sold them as Chinese Snake Oil.

We still see quack medicine, particularly online. TikTok is famous for sharing ridiculous, sometimes dangerous, health information. I won't get into the TikTok challenges which aren't disinformation as much as people doing really stupid things. Many experts have taken to TikTok and other media to dispel the disinformation that is shared.

There are even more examples of disinformation in health care. Think about diseases throughout history. Initially, the Black Plague (Black Death, Bubonic Plague) was thought to be divine intervention. God was pissed off at people because they sinned. This was (and in some circles still is) the narrative that surrounded the HIV/AIDS epidemic. Because it was so focused on one marginalized community (homosexuals), it was considered God bringing the plague to such sinners. Absent sound science, these narratives persisted and persist yet today.

If you look at older advertising, you may see ads for alcohol and cigarettes marketing both products as good for you. We have since come to realize that cigarettes can kill you and alcohol is fine in moderation. Given what we knew at the time, even doctors recommended alcohol and smoking. We now know better, but the narrative is already out there. It's sometimes difficult to take back.

Often politics and not science drive our narratives (more on this in Chapter 2). Think about the current narrative around gun control in the US. We have data that indicate that when we banned assault-type weapons, gun violence decreased 25 percent. That's significant. Yet some will have you believe that more guns mean increased safety. I even had a colleague tell me that he thinks teachers and professors should be armed. That is his answer (and others) to the incidences of mass shootings in schools. I have given myself a name in case it ever comes to that: Pistol Packing Professor Pauline (huge fan of alliteration).

While the term "infodemic" is relatively new, disinformation has been with us for centuries. We've been lying to each other as long as we've been communicating with each other. We have also been trying to understand the world around us and have used science to help.

# I Can't Tell An Atom From An Anus

## The Scientific Method Explained

**BEFORE WE CONTINUE** a conversation about the infodemic, it's important to understand how "science" works. I put "science" in quotation marks because science isn't the only discipline that used a methodical approach to decision-making and discovery.

People have a skewed view of what science is. I want to clarify that this doesn't just apply to science or how you might strictly define science. Usually when I think of or reference science, I and others think of the "hard" sciences like biology, chemistry, and physics. Yes, those are natural sciences. There are also social sciences of which communication is a part. What I want to get everyone to consider is that the scientific method can be used to think critically and help us to solve problems—big and small. I often use it to sort through problems. Honestly, I think I do it without realizing I am using it. You probably do as well.

Another misconception people seem to have is that once scientists have done an experiment and they have their findings, it's done. Finished. Conclusion reached. Nothing more needs to be said.

Sometimes. Perhaps. Maybe.

Sometimes not. In this chapter, I'll explain how science works, particularly how scientists formulate ideas and test those ideas to see if they are sound.

## SCIENCE IS SOCIAL

Science is a social process. It is never complete, and it is never perfect. I think there is an expectation that it be complete and perfect. Certainty is an illusion. Remember this. It will return to haunt us throughout this book.

Can we say the same thing in other areas of our lives? Have you ever researched something—and I don't mean administered a survey or conducted a focus group or worked in a lab—I mean, for example, have you ever looked at an online review of a restaurant? You see many very good reviews, so you go to the restaurant. You have a bad experience. Your soup was lukewarm, and you didn't get crackers. Do you return? Perhaps you think to yourself that online reviews can't all be wrong. The reviews noted that people got crackers. And the good kind—not the cheap saltines knockoffs. Perhaps you went during lunch, but you should have gone during dinner? Perhaps you went on Tuesday and Thursday is the better day? Perhaps you just got a cranky server, or the chef was off her game. Perhaps they were out of crackers. You try again. And again. How often will you return if you have bad experiences? Does one good review counterweigh the others? Have you read all the reviews? Have you written one?

That's one example, and you may argue that it is ridiculous and isn't "scientific." I would agree to a point. I mean, it's not biology. Think about what the scientific method is intended to do.

Let's look at a political example. Are you familiar with the term "flip-flop?" Yes, it's a casual sandal, but I mean flip-flopping on an issue. It occurs when a politician may have voted one way in the past and now votes another way. Or when that politician said one thing in the past and has now said another, or said the opposite. That person will be accused of flip-flopping. It is meant to be derogatory.

It could be that the politician is pandering. It could also be that she got additional information that wasn't available when she made her initial decision. That information has caused her to see things in a different way. She changed her mind based on new and better data. That's also flip-flopping. I hope you change your mind if you are presented with new and better information to allow you to now make a more informed choice, but that's me. Some of us are stubborn.

When we became aware of Covid-19 there were so many unanswered questions. Scientists knew much but were still figuring things out, such as how long does the virus survive outside the body? Does it survive on hard surfaces like the kitchen counter? What are the long-term effects of the virus? The last question we are still trying to figure out because it seems to vary so widely from person to person. We know much but not everything. Certainty is an illusion.

I think that gives people pause. If scientists don't know or if they keep "changing their minds" what does that mean for the rest of us?

We've seen this historically as I've mentioned. When your doctor recommends smoking and booze, well, changing that narrative is difficult when there is new and better information. Smoking and booze may be pleasurable. Think of the numerous studies we see related to wine, coffee, artificial sweeteners, etc. One year they are good for us; the next they are not. It appears science flip-flops.

Let's go back to Covid-19. I, too, didn't know what to make of Covid-19 when it first surfaced. I told students they were likely safe because it seemed to impact older adults and those with co-morbidities and pre-existing conditions. When I realized I was wrong, I corrected the narrative. I flip-flopped and shared more accurate information with my students. I admitted I had been wrong, but given the information I had at the time, it's what I concluded. I flip-flopped. I admitted I was wrong.

## THE SCIENTIFIC METHOD

All of this means we need to understand science and how it works. Allow me to list the steps in the scientific method—followed by every scientist (generally, I don't like to use such inclusive words as "every" or "all," but in this case I think every and all scientists use the scientific method). Do you remember learning the steps of this method? If not, here's a refresher:

- Have a question
- Research that question
- Form a hypothesis
- Experiment
- Analyze data
- Draw conclusions (and share)

These steps are the framework you can (and should) use when following this method. Let's dig into each one.

## Have a Question and Research It

You must have a question to start. How is Covid-19 transmitted? How does disinformation start? Why do people believe things they see online? Then you can start to do some secondary research, which is all about finding information that's already out there that might help you with your question. Have others tried to answer your question? If they haven't answered the question, have they done something that might help you advance information on the topic? What background knowledge is out there that may help you decide how to advance knowledge on the topic in question?

## Form a Hypothesis

Let's use an example we may all understand. Let's also forget for a moment that we already know the answer to this question. Suppose I want a house plant. I see this great peace lily at the farmers' market. I am interested in how often I should water the plant and how much water I should give it for maximum growth—or to keep it alive. I do some research online via my smart phone and ask the farmer for insight. I hypothesize that I will need to water the plant at least once per week. Now I craft my experiment.

## Experiment

I buy three plants because I am serious about this. I am interested in water only, so I want to make sure I keep all other variables and conditions the same. I put all three plants in the same window (it's a large window ledge). That way they have the same amount of light and are in the same part of the room. I control any other variables or things that may affect my plant.

I water all three plants with a half a cup of water. I want to get them all started on the right footing. Now I make changes. Plant one gets a half a cup of water once per week. Plant two gets a half a cup of water every other week. Plant three gets no water.

I observe what happens. It is probably something like this: plant one flourishes. It is green and has several flowers. Plant two is okay, but has some brown patches on its leaves and no flowers. Plant three is dead in a month.

A simple experiment I used here for explanatory purposes. There would be a bit more to it than I've outlined, but I think you get the point well enough. First, I had a question: "How often should I water my plant for maximum growth?" Then I researched that question via Google and the farmer. I formed a hypothesis: "The plant will require watering once per week with half a cup of water to ensure optimal growth." I conducted my experiment by buying three plants and adjusting the watering of each. I analyzed my data: Plant one looks great, plant two needs some help, plant three is now compost. I drew conclusions and shared with my friends on Instagram and perhaps that farmer (who now thinks I am an idiot).

What if my hypothesis was watering every other week? Am I a failure? I disproved my hypothesis, but I still learned something. Some scientists forget that there is no failing in science. There is always knowledge. You learn something whether it's what you expected or not.

Experiments may be conducted in several ways. You may administer a survey, or you may read online reviews. You may conduct scientific studies. You may conduct the experiment as I outlined above.

Something else you may have heard in relation to Covid-19 or other health and science research is a double-blind study. This is the gold standard in scientific research. Simply, a double-blind study involves two groups—one that receives the treatment and one that does not (called a control). The researcher does not know who is getting the "treatment" and who is in the control group; nor does the individual in the test.

An example of a double-blind study might be a taste test. I, as the researcher, may put different drinks in different unlabeled cups. The person conducting the experiment doesn't know which cup contains which drink nor does the person sampling the drinks. This ensures as unbiased a taste test as possible. Coca-Cola and Pepsi used to have taste tests that made for fun in the neighborhood. We always said we could tell the difference. I honestly don't remember if we could.

Double-blind studies also help to account for the placebo effect. There is research that notes that if people are ill and they are given a treatment, they may get well whether that treatment is legitimate or not. We "will" ourselves better—the placebo effect. This doesn't happen to everyone, but it does happen to some.

An example investigating the placebo effect may occur when testing medications. The researcher randomly places subjects into groups— one gets the experimental medication and one gets a "placebo" or no medication. The subject and researcher have no idea who is in which group either. Some subjects will improve with the medication; some will also improve with the placebo. Ideally, those receiving the medication improve statistically significantly over those receiving the placebo, otherwise the hypothesis is not supported.

## Analyze Data

After any experiment is conducted, you need to analyze your data. When doing so, it is important to remove as many of your own biases as possible. I would argue you will never remove all biases from anything, but you must do your best. Why do I say this? I've worked with companies who explain away findings to suit themselves and they use data to justify it. Data don't lie; people may lie when interpreting it—and not necessarily intentionally. For example, if I am looking for the source of a particular piece of disinformation I found online, I might find that it came from a large evil Satanic cult that is trying to take over the world one social post at a time (this could be true—I've not conducted experiments). I don't want this to be true because we are all doomed against Satan, so I try to explain my findings by saying that it is just a bunch of fraternity boys in their basement playing games. I'm not looking at my data objectively and I am stereotyping fraternity boys.

## Draw Conclusion and Share Findings

Sometimes it helps to have an outside pair of eyes look at your data— someone who doesn't have a horse in the race, so to speak. I often look at data for people. I look at the data and before I offer my feedback, I always ask them what they see. Sometimes I agree; sometimes I don't. It is always interesting to me how people who have some skin in the game interpret data to suit their own needs. Most of the time it's in justifying why the data present as they do. People want an explanation and someone or something to blame if the results aren't roses and sunshine. The latest scapegoat? Covid-19. "Oh, we got those results saying that everyone hates our company because of Covid-19." Um, I'm looking at the data and see that everyone thinks the CEO is an arse. I don't think that's Covid-19.

This is also where peer review comes into play. I think people often feel as though scientists conduct an experiment and then tell the world or get it published easily. Not so fast. Scientists must write up their findings in the form of a scientific paper (abstract, introduction, methodology, results, discussion, conclusions, references) and then submit said paper to a reputable journal or other outlet (generally an academic journal). That report is written in scientific jargon. It isn't intended for a lay audience. Nerds like me read papers like this. It is submitted blind, meaning researchers' names are not included on the paper. This is done to eliminate—again, as much bias as possible. Every journal has reviewers who are experts in the field the journal is intended for. For example, the *Journal of Communication* would have communication researchers review studies; the *Journal of the American Medical Association* would have medical people review studies. These reviewers are looking to make sure you have cited the appropriate information in your introduction; that your methodology makes sense given what you are trying to study; that your results seem to follow what you did; that your discussion and conclusions make sense; that your references are appropriate.

Sharing your findings might be the most important part of the scientific method. Why? Remember our first two steps? Ask a question and do some secondary research? Your findings become secondary research for the next researcher. If you conduct your experiment and then squirrel away your findings, you deprive science of your insights. That could set things back. Science and research should be a collaborative, collective, cooperative endeavor.

If you patronize that restaurant and have a bad experience when others have had good ones, you should write that review. Share your findings.

How would you use the scientific method with our restaurant review situation? I don't think you would sit down with the list I've used above and go point by point, but let me do that for you as an example:

- **Have a question.** *Will I like this restaurant?*
- **Research that question.** Read reviews of the restaurant. *They are generally good and focus on what I care about—food and service.*
- **Form a hypothesis.** *I will like this restaurant.*
- **Experiment.** Go to the restaurant ten different times. Vary the day of the week and time of day. Order soup each time.
- **Analyze data.** *Did I like it? Those bastards didn't give me crackers and the soup was lukewarm.* I returned several times and didn't like it any of those times. This at least shows reiteration. You don't want to base findings on one person or one review—what scientists call an N of 1. N is the number of people or iterations of an experiment.
- **Draw conclusions (and share).** *I did not like this restaurant and will add my review to the website.*

As I mentioned, you likely go through the above steps subconsciously. Perhaps you write them down as I did but not likely. But you are using the scientific method. To be fair, you aren't going to be as deliberate and methodical. Ten times and soup each time? Come on.

Science is an evolution (science also studies evolution, but I digress). We learn from one another. The next researcher may take my findings of the Satanic cult overtaking the world and do additional research and find that it isn't a bunch of fraternity boys but a well-organized disinformation machine from XYZ country intent on sowing confusion and chaos.

## WHAT FINDINGS CAN YOU TRUST?

Communication is also key in all of this (said the communication professor). It is important that it be communicated that what you are reporting is one step in the process and it's what we know right now. We reserve the right to modify our findings based on new information. New information may always come along.

Let's go back to Covid-19 as an example. We knew early on that the virus was transmitted in the air. We urged people to wear masks and practice social distancing. Once vaccines were available, we encouraged everyone who could safely get vaccinated to get vaccinated. Are there side effects with vaccines? There could be. There are side effects with most drugs/vaccines. I don't think it was communicated well enough that getting vaccinated doesn't mean you won't get Covid-19 (I did get it having been vaccinated and boosted). It just means you won't suffer the same effects as if you hadn't been vaccinated. We know much about Covid-19, but still don't know everything.

This may also be a case of scientists and health care folks thinking people knew more about vaccines than they do. Again, we are assuming scientists can share their knowledge and skills. We know they're safe, but did we explain that well enough? I don't think we did.

We also need to look at our global response to Covid-19 because more pandemics are coming (not an exaggeration or an "end of the world" statement). What can and would we do differently the next time? Do you see how this becomes a loop? We go back to the start and continue to ask questions, do the research, form hypotheses, experiment, analyze, and conclude. Rinse and repeat—that's how science works and evolves.

I think Covid-19 uncovered and highlighted for us a lack of science and health literacy. That lack of information has sown the seeds of disinformation around Covid, vaccines, health care, science, and more.

Let's go back to the restaurant example for a moment to further illustrate this point. What's missing from that example? Any semblance of peer review. In fact, I caution people when looking at online reviews because this is where disinformation may also exist. It's sometimes difficult to tell if a review is from a legitimate person or a so-called bot. It's also hard to determine if unbiased patrons wrote the review or if the owner got all his friends to do so. You could dig deeply into the reviews to find out who people are, or you could take your chances. Admittedly, this is a rather innocuous example.

To ensure scientific studies are done well and within the guidelines of science, we have regulatory bodies like the Food and Drug Administration (FDA) in the United States. Scientists also present their findings to peer-reviewed journals. The journal articles are peer reviewed without knowing who the authors are to prevent, as much as possible, reviewer bias.

That said, not all journals are the same. Each field of study, whether it's communication or business or chemistry or psychology, has what it considers "top-tier journals." Those are journals that are extremely difficult to get published in because the standards are very high. That is not to say that those journals not in the top tier are "less than," but researchers strive for the best of the best. Don't we all? I say that to remind you that you need to do your due diligence. Just because something was published in an academic "journal" does not automatically make it a seminal study. Does it add to present research? Likely. Often when you see the news media reference an academic study, you see that it appeared in a top-tier journal.

The same may be said in other areas. I am a writer and I work with journalists. I have penned several editorials for newspapers. Is there a tier system among newspapers? Yes. I have written for my local and hyper-local newspapers and have had my editorials published. I have not written for the *The New York Times* or *The Guardian*, for example. A peer review exists here also. Just because I've written something doesn't mean it gets published. An editorial staff reviews submissions and publishes those it deems worthy and have met editorial standards. Generally, they look to make sure you have some authority and appropriate credentials with which to speak, in addition to a timely topic.

What about this book? Is it peer reviewed? I'm not sharing a draft with any of my academic peers. That said, I had to draft a book proposal, which was then sent to a legitimate publisher (Broad Book Press) who checked to make sure I had the street cred (expertise) to write about this topic and the ability to write and communicate. They could have said, "thank you, next."

Are studies ever approved, written up, presented for review, and printed? Yes. Are they ever found later to be wrong? Yes. The best example is the study done by physician Andrew Wakefield on a group of twelve people that appeared in the prestigious medical journal, *The Lancet*, in 1998. Twelve people. I don't want to get into statistics and research methodology here, but twelve people do not a study make. If you go to *The Lancet*'s site, you will see **RETRACTED** printed across this article.

Keep in mind that a retraction is generally issued if there is something wrong with the methodology or results. The conclusions drawn from the results would also be suspect, but given what was "found," the leap to the conclusions may not be so odd. In the case of the debunked study that suggested vaccines cause autism, the number of respondents was one of the things found to be problematic. Another recent case involved a scientist manipulating data. Those things are career enders. Marc Tessier-Lavigne, president of Stanford University, was forced to resign his position amid allegations that he manipulated data on several scientific studies. Oops. The same thing happens in other areas in which we level trust in someone. More on trust later.

A retraction is great, but *The Lancet* article helped catalyze a movement against vaccines. It also highlights that no matter what new information you have, you will have those who won't flip-flop and will hang onto whatever they believe to be true. Retractions are important but can also be dangerous. They may help sow distrust. We all make mistakes, but we expect certain professions to be free of them.

## THE CHANGING LANDSCAPE OF SCIENCE

People also may have a sense of distrust because science "changes." It does, but...the basic tenets are generally the same. If you look at science and medicine throughout history, you will see that we have believed some crazy things. I would argue that we believed crazy things before we had any idea how to truly measure and study them.

Let's look at an example from health care history. Coca-Cola did once contain actual cocaine. In the late 1800s–early 1900s, cocaine was legal and was considered safe in small quantities, like that present in Coca-Cola. Originally, Coca-Cola was sold as a "brain tonic and intellectual beverage." I bet there were plenty of stimulating conversations had by intellectuals who consumed it. What changed? Science and time. Whoops, turns out cocaine is dangerous even in small quantities. It's no longer in Coca-Cola, so don't get excited.

Here's another example. Before physicians knew much about women, any unexplained medical problem was dubbed "hysteria." That is, any problem a woman presented to her doctor that didn't fit the usual symptoms was just dumped into the hysteria bucket. The cure? Genital stimulation with a vibrator. Yes, you read that correctly. The late 1800s–early 1900s may have been a good time to be alive for women!

Now we know the problem is much more involved than "hysteria." Women and other marginalized groups haven't been taken seriously in many areas of life, and health care is just one. How does that play into our understanding of disinformation? Wait and see.

Science works because it has its own checks and balances. It is peer reviewed. It is communicated and debated. Once a study has been published in a legitimate academic journal (or other respected area), it may be debated by other experts. It may also have gotten there because there is scientific consensus on the topic. There may be some uncertainty that is open to debate and additional research. Generally speaking, you don't have fringe ideas finding their way into legitimate academic journals. That's what the internet and social media are for.

And that's where some disinformation starts.

Where does that leave us?

You don't need to understand science to be able to use the scientific method. You don't need to know the difference between an atom and an anus (though if you were to search, I would suggest Googling atom first).

I will return to the scientific method throughout this book. It is important.

First, let me return to Covid-19 for a moment. Why did there seem to be such a misunderstanding about this disease and why was it communicated as such? It has been suggested that with Covid-19, the world was able to see the scientific method in action. The public was able to pull the curtain from around the wizard and see the gadgets deployed. We were able to get inside the heads of the best scientific and medical minds and have access to the stream of consciousness that flows in all directions around a scientific question. It was at once fascinating and dangerous. It led to some of the disinformation and distrust we saw around the pandemic. It may also have tainted science and medicine for years to come. Are scientists, doctors, and academics charlatans? We were able to see our inability to create a common narrative—at least at first.

When we discuss science, we often hear a counter discussion about faith and whether the two are mutually exclusive. Can you both believe and know? We can look to history for evidence of this intellectual conflict. Charles Darwin himself had trouble postulating his theory of evolution because he was a Christian man. It conflicted with his belief that God created the world. He faced much criticism from fellow scientists because they too believed in the creation myth. He was pilloried in life. But look at how far he's come! [Full disclosure: I own a copy of the collected works of Darwin which includes *On the Origin of Species* because...of course I do.]

In distinguishing between science and faith, I would also like to distinguish between science and politics. They are **not** the same. Politics is not often driven by science. We saw that quite clearly during the Covid-19 pandemic. We saw politicians recommending and legislating policies and practices that moved counter to what science knew and recommended. I think Dr. Anthony Fauci had a full head of brown hair in 2020—that is now gray and receding. I say that in jest because I often saw him and others grit their teeth and express disdain at the politicization of the pandemic.

Science may also be used to justify hate and violence. We saw that in the Holocaust when the Nazis used "science" to justify who was fit to live and who should die. Again, politics conflict with science. Sadly, too often people equate the two which doesn't help scientists, nor does it help infodemiologists.

## WORDS MATTER

In discussing the scientific method, it is also important to discuss nomenclature. What do I mean by that? Essentially what we name stuff. This also may help to explain the scientific method and how science is a process.

Let's start with climate change. If you are more seasoned (that means "older") like me, you likely remember when it was called "global warming." Why? When climate change was first detected it was because we noticed gradually warming seas and glacial and polar ice cap melt. That signaled to the scientific community that the globe was warming, hence the moniker "global warming." We have since realized—through additional research and exploration—that warming is just the tip of the iceberg (puns are always intended). In addition to warming seas and melting polar ice caps, we see more extreme weather events, and species extinctions or species migrations, that we hadn't seen in the past. They are getting worse. As I type this, wildfires are raging across Canada and blanketing parts of the United States with a dangerous smog. Global warming as a name wasn't going to cut it anymore.

The problem with this is that many people remember when it was called global warming and use that to ridicule the updated science. They may say things like, "Oh, global warming yet we just had a blizzard." Names and words do matter.

A political example? Defund the police. That phrase and that movement are intended to draw attention to the disproportionate number of people of color who are targeted and/or killed by the police. It is intended to offer alternatives to weaponized and militarized police systems. It doesn't mean taking all the taxpayer money away from police and have no system of order whatsoever. Yet...that's exactly what that phrase looks like. Names and words do matter.

Another favorite of mine? I will use a pop-culture reference. When Gwyneth Paltrow announced that she and Chris Martin were divorcing, she used the phrase "conscious uncoupling," which is a phrase coined by Katherine Woodward Thomas to describe, essentially, an amicable breakup. My first thought was, "Okay, I've broken up with people and I've done so quite consciously. I've never been in a coma and broken up with someone." Yes, I know I am looking at this literally, but that's what people do. Names and words do matter.

What about the term "organic?" For a scientist, organic refers to any compound containing carbon. That's pretty much all life forms. What does "organic" mean to a consumer? Most assume it means produce produced without fertilizers or pesticides. However, that isn't always true. Then you have the term "natural." I don't even want to get into "grass-fed," "free-range," "cage-free."

These examples help to highlight the struggle the scientific community faces when they find new and better/different information after having presented something. In fact, some have said that Covid-19 provided the perfect view behind the curtain to see the wizard in action. In other words, we saw science uncloaked and raw. We saw scientists using the scientific method, testing hypotheses, drawing conclusions, communicating findings and then modifying and updating those conclusions, and so on and so on. That didn't sit well with many.

We should also think about the power we give to science. When we talk to people about science and scientific discoveries, we should be careful not to say we've "proven" something. Remember that science is neither complete nor perfect. Certainty is an illusion. Science is intended to explain not to persuade. Persuasion is the job of others, but they may refer to science to justify the persuasion. Science also relies on consensus. If someone is sharing a fringe idea, be suspect.

# "If It's On The Internet It Must Be True"

## And Other Lies We Tell Ourselves

**YOU MAY BE FAMILIAR** with famous people—we may call them influencers—who are being used by disinformationists to disseminate false and dangerous information. Two examples come to mind.

You may recall that Damar Hamlin is the Buffalo Bills safety who suffered a cardiac incident live on a Monday night football game on January 2, 2023. Luckily, Mr. Hamlin is recovering well. It is still unclear what caused the cardiac arrest, but one thing medical professionals seem to agree on is that it is not a result of the Covid-19 (or any) vaccine.

Another example is Grant Wahl, the CBS sports journalist who was covering the World Cup in Qatar in 2022 when he suffered a ruptured aortic aneurysm. His widow, Céline Gounder, an infectious disease specialist and epidemiologist, has written that she knew his death could be used as disinformation fodder, so she had an autopsy performed by top pathologists and forensic scientists. (If you have not read her excellent editorial in *The New York Times*, please do.[8])

In both cases, in the absence of immediate answers, there was a rush to judgment. And the poison-penned were the first on the scene. Their playground for misinformation? The internet, of course. In this chapter, I'll dive into our assumptions about what "must" be true in relation to where we read or hear about it.

## CORRELATION DOES NOT NECESSARILY EQUAL CAUSATION

It is no surprise to those of us who study conspiracies and disinformation that high-profile people would be used to push a false and dangerous agenda. That doesn't make it any less disturbing or dangerous. Dr. Gounder details in her editorial the tactics used by those creating and sharing disinformation. It's a common playbook and one I'll discuss shortly.

First, let's consider what Dr. Gounder thought. She's mourning the death of her husband but has the presence of mind and inclination to note what people will assume. Brilliant…and a sad commentary. It is a prebuttal, though. More on that later.

It's easy to blame these incidents on something like the Covid-19 vaccine. Detractors could (and will) say that, "We don't really know, so it's obviously the vaccine." Um, I guess, but there are many other things in common. They are both men. Perhaps it's because they are men that they suffered like this. They are both involved in football (one American and one global). I think football might be the problem. I saw them both in pictures wearing T-shirts. Everyone buy sweaters!

I say these things half in jest. We nerds call these spurious correlations. We want to say that A and B happened, and because A happened first, it must have caused B. That could be the case, but let's take a closer look at what we are trying to explain. Do the variables make sense together? So, (A) both of these gentlemen received the vaccine, and (B) before their medical crises. Therefore, A is the cause of B. And, (A) both of these men wore T-shirts, (B) before their medical crises. Therefore, A is the cause of B.

**TIP**

If you want to see spurious correlations in action, please visit www.tylervigen.com[9] and have some fun. I often have my students look at this site as an example of what not to do. They don't all always get that and some of them honestly try to explain the "correlations." For example, the more people who consume cheese, the more people die by getting tangled in their bedsheets. I had a student once explain that as, "well, if you eat too much cheese you become lethargic and aren't as able to untangle yourself from your sheets." No. Spurious at best.

Of course, sometimes A does cause B. We must be very careful about making those assumptions or connecting those dots. That's where science and the scientific method come in. Let's look at Mr. Hamlin. As of this writing, we do not know definitively what caused his cardiac arrest. There are many very plausible and scientifically backed explanations that are being explored. Does he have an underlying condition that predisposes him? Did he get hit in the chest in the one-in-a-million way that would cause this?

Could it be the Covid-19 vaccine? That would be difficult to prove. What is known is that the vaccine has been tested and administered to millions of people. There are side effects, but the side effects reported are not cardiac arrest and aortic aneurysm. Generally speaking, side effects associated with the vaccine would be noticed sooner rather than months later, and would affect more than one or two people.

More importantly, let's think about the efficacy of vaccines. Vaccines save lives. While it is still possible to contract Covid even if vaccinated, your chances of becoming critically ill and/or hospitalized are greatly decreased. That's true of most vaccines. Historically, vaccines have prevented us from getting many deadly diseases like smallpox, measles, and flu.

## THE POWER OF INFLUENCE

Let me transition to a discussion of using "influencers" to push your agenda. One post from an influential person can spread to millions of people in seconds. Think about the number of people who were following the story of both Mr. Wahl and Mr. Hamlin. Millions of people. Both stories were so incredible and were shared widely, including by many well-known influential people. And when that happens, the result can often be a sharing (whether intentional or not) of inaccurate information on a global scale.

Justin Trudeau, prime minister of Canada, saw this power of influence firsthand in 2022 when he posted about Iran. He Tweeted:

"Canada denounces the Iranian regime's barbaric decision to impose the death penalty on nearly 15,000 protesters," the English tweet said. "These brave Iranians were fighting for their human rights—and we continue to stand united in support of them, and united against the regime's heinous actions."

The problem is that the number of people for whom the death penalty was imposed was greatly exaggerated. Trudeau's team took the Tweet down after about twelve hours. His account had 6.3 million followers at the time. That Tweet was shared by Viola Davis, actress and producer, who had 1.8 million followers at the time. When Trudeau removed the Tweet, it remained on Davis's account. Certainly 6.3 million and 1.8 million people didn't see that Tweet, nor did they share it, but they could have. That's just two people. Think about the reach beyond just those two individuals.

This was a case of misinformation. Trudeau's team thought they had accurate information. When they realized they didn't, they removed it. Davis trusted information coming from Trudeau, so she shared it. And so on and so on.

Another example highlights how the media and others may be their own worst enemies. Rapper Nicki Minaj tweeted in September 2021:

"My cousin in Trinidad won't get the vaccine cuz his friend got it & became impotent. His testicles became swollen. His friend was weeks away from getting married, now the girl called off the wedding. So just pray on it & make sure you're comfortable with ur decision, not bullied."

At the time she had about 22 million followers (she now has over 27 million). That Tweet has been retweeted 23,600 times, quoted 88,800 times, liked 139,900 times, and bookmarked 7,389 times (as of this writing). Without doing a more extensive analysis of the spread of the

Tweet, this is powerful. Those who retweeted may have had their retweet retweeted, liked, etc.

The media coverage that this one Tweet generated is also noteworthy. It was covered in numerous media outlets each with its own followers who likely shared, liked, and bookmarked it. The Trinidadian Health Minister and others spoke out against the Tweet. Think about the reach the backlash alone garnered. I don't have those numbers, but I must believe it is considerable. I don't listen to her music, nor do I follow her account, but I am aware of it (yes, I study this, but still).

Even if information is deleted, it is still there. The modern adage of "if it's private don't post it" is real.

## THE MOTIVATION TO SHARE DISINFORMATION

What do people click on and share? Why do people create and share? In the case of Trudeau, it was an honest mistake. For many people it may be. We live in a time when the number of likes, shares, and followers determines the worth of many of us. If we create something that is saucy, it is likely to get shared, which may increase the number of our followers which, in turn, might help to make us an influencer. What we do and say will garner attention for us.

We are also motived by fear. Often that fear exists because we have an information void. We are missing necessary information, and whatever appeals to our fears and fills that void, is what we are going to pay attention to.

The language that is used is also important. What words or phrases are used? What memes? Are we hitting on cultural milestones that resonate? Are we also relying on those in our sphere of influence—those who we deem to have some sort of power (remember our discussion of the six types of power in Chapter 1).

While there were many stories circulated during the pandemic that contained disinformation, there were also many stories that were helpful. Medical professionals in each case came forward to help explain what was going on, provide insights, and in some cases, tips to prevent the same fate from befalling you. That's taking a horrible situation and finding the good (of course the educator writing this will say that education is good).

There are also several outlets, organizations, individuals, and groups that formed because of the disinformation around the pandemic. This author is one example with her podcast, blog, and now book. There are others (see Chapter 10 for more).

Take a look at what disinformationists are doing. They see a chance to push their agendas. They may make money. They may become influencers or demi-Gods. The bottom line, be careful of spurious claims. Look at what science, from actual scientists, has to say.

You might argue that I am a communication professional who has worked in health care for ages but who isn't a medical doctor. Correct. You might also argue that I have no business commenting on medical issues. Wrong. Where do I get my information? I regularly speak with experts in the field, and I read, watch, and listen. I am constantly educating myself. Remember that one of my skills is taking medical and scientific information and distilling it for people. That is my "authority."

## HOW DISINFORMATIONISTS SUCK YOU IN

What do disinformationists do to suck you in? They use several tactics to create and disseminate information. There are many tactics designed to persuade. One of my favorite graphics is **Disinformation 101** in **Figure 2**. It details very well many of the actions used by disinformationists. Let's break some of them down.

### Fake "Experts"

The logical fallacy of using fake experts involves "presenting unqualified individuals or institutions as sources of credible information." Within this category you may see the bulking of fake experts, magnifying the minority, or producing a fake debate. What do we mean?

Bulking fake experts isn't the same thing as "9 out of 10 dentists prefer...." but it's close. You might see a social media post noting that "most" doctors think a particular way that seems counter to what "mainstream media" is telling you. Often you see "most" or "many" without any actual

**FIGURE 2:** Disinformation 101

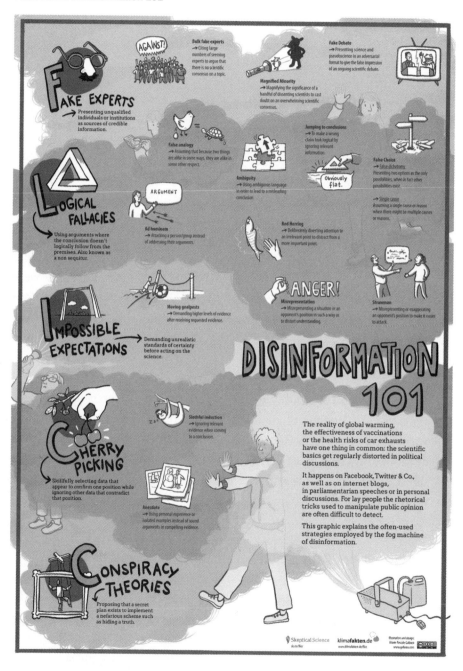

number. It is being made to seem as though there is a silent majority that isn't being heard but is now being magnified. FYI: there is no silent majority.

## Groupthink

Groupthink works in a similar way. This is when a group "decides" together because they think they all agree, and that dissent is not possible. Generally, you aren't alone. Someone will believe as you do but, like you, doesn't want to make the first move.

You may also feel as though so many more people feel a certain way than not. I can use a personal example. I decided in my "day job" that I wasn't popular with everyone. That is to be expected. If you try to please everyone, you please no one, as they say. (As a note, you should be careful of the "they" in "they say" because we don't know who "they" are.) I was ripped apart on Facebook. It felt as though thousands of people were against my decision because the minority had such a voice. It turned out there were about ten people who were upset. As I said, I thought it was thousands.

## False Debates

A fake debate is like bulking fake experts in that it seems to pit these expert groups against one another. The silent majority is attacking the vocal majority. Again, there is no silent majority. There may be some dissenters, but they are few. When scientists and others determine through the scientific method (I said it wouldn't go away) that something is true, there may be a few who question it and/or want to do more research but there is generally no debate that would upend what was determined.

## Ad Hominem Attacks

Logical fallacies like redirection and ad hominem attacks are common. "Using arguments where the conclusion doesn't logically follow from the premises," is a logical fallacy. We often see logical fallacies used to discredit the sharer and/or creator of information. For example, an ad hominem attack would be used to steer the debate away from the issues and rather to the person. For example, I may tell you that the sky is blue and someone sharing disinformation may retort that I can't be trusted because I am tall and tall people don't know things. My being tall has nothing to do with whether I can discern the sky's color.

We also see ad hominem attacks that are used to rile a group to action. More and more we are seeing people hide behind the anonymity of social media to pillory people who have spoken out against something or someone. Often that vitriol comes because the person issues an ad hominem attack. The response is quite vicious. Some report receiving death threats against themselves or friends and family. The anonymity of the internet allows for people to say things they may not say if they were in front of you. That said, it's important to remember that on the other side of the social media account or newspaper article or other piece is a human being. Would you want your mother, brother, or daughter to be the target of such attacks? No? Then don't subject anyone to them. Civility should remain. (Though optimism may not.)

## Ambiguity

I may also be ambiguous in my explanation. This may include using ambiguous language like the famous Groucho Marx joke, "One morning I shot an elephant in my pajamas. How he got into my pajamas I'll never know." Did Marx literally mean the elephant was wearing his pajamas or that he was when he shot said elephant? Ambiguity.

## False Analogies and Conclusions

How about a false analogy? We see these all the time if you think about how stereotypes are formed. Also, in how people sometimes form opinions. Let's look at the 2020 election. I saw a gentleman comment in the media that he knows Donald J. Trump won because all his friends voted for him. How could Biden have won? This analogy precludes the people you don't know. It lumps everyone together into one common group—a group which may not be so common.

Jumping to false conclusions is another tactic used by spreaders of disinformation. There are different facets to jumping to conclusions, but generally it is forming an opinion without all relevant information and assuming that opinion applies more broadly than it does. I may assume that all those who didn't want to get the Covid-19 vaccine are Republicans because so many are, and I've seen them! (hyperbole for effect, dear reader). The truth is much more complex. Yes, data do support this statement, but...there are also other groups who did not get vaccinated for several reasons. See Chapter 5. Jumping to conclusions is easy to do and dangerous.

## Red Herrings

The red herring is another fallacy and not a delicacy. I often hear the term used in politics and it isn't always used correctly. Big surprise. A red herring is diverting one's attention away from the topic at hand to perhaps a more salacious topic. How many times have you watched candidates debate without actually answering the question? The moderator may ask, "How do you plan to combat disinformation stemming from social media platforms," and the candidate may reply with, "I have an excellent approach to combating disinformation on social media and I also have a plan to reduce inflation. Let me explain my three-pronged approach to decreasing gas prices." The candidate mildly addressed the question and then went onto something else. A red herring. It made you think the question was being addressed but the person went in a different direction.

## False Choices

We will end this section on logical fallacies by addressing false choices. There are two main types: single cause and false dichotomy. A single cause fallacy makes it seem as though there is just one answer to a problem when there may be many. Arguing that climate change is caused by greenhouse gas emissions is one example. Yes, that is a cause, but there are others. A false dichotomy presents you with two choices when there are, indeed, more than two. "You are either for us or against us," is a perfect example. "If you didn't get the Covid-19 vaccine you must be stupid." Not even close.

To understand false choices, you need to understand how selective information plays into the narrative. Let's do some cherry picking, and I don't mean climbing ladders to get to the fantastic fruit. British Economist Ronald Coase once said, "Torture the data, and it will confess to anything." Anyone may find what they are looking for in the data if they dig and manipulate long and hard enough. You may see a news article that focuses quite heavily on one side of an issue, while ignoring other sides of it. I will detail in Chapter 6 how you may recognize when the media does this. Cherry picking is like slothful induction in that the latter just ignores other information that is out there; cherry picking sifts through it to get to the information to bolster your argument. The retracted *The Lancet* journal article referenced earlier noting that vaccines cause autism is a perfect example. They don't, yet many still believe they do. They ignore all other information, ignore the retraction, and cling to this false information. My favorite fallacy is the anecdote. I call it the "N of one" fallacy. (N refers to the number of people or iterations in a study—your sample size. I won't get into the statistics around determining sample size but suffice to say that a sample size of one is not good.) We have all heard about our grandfather or grandmother (or whomever) who drank a bottle of wine and smoked two packs of cigarettes a day and lived to 100, so how can booze and smokes be bad? Good on nana and papa, but not for the whole.

## Impossible Expectations

Impossible expectations are often used to stymie information but setting the burden of proof at a high level, prevents those in the know from countering an argument. If I say that I will get the Covid-19 vaccine when it is 100 percent effective, I will never get it. Nothing is 100 percent. I could misrepresent the argument to gain followers, for example. Colin Kaepernick kneeling for the national anthem was widely misrepresented as an anti-patriotic stance. By his own admission he was using his platform to speak out against violence against his race. Many used it as an opportunity to paint those who peacefully protest in this manner as anti-American. A misrepresentation. Creating a narrative that suggests that I, as the author of this book, am incapable of building a house and, therefore, you shouldn't read the book is building a strawman to detract from my real skills and talents in writing, and determine what should be included in this book.

That's a very simple walk through of logical fallacies used to create and spread disinformation. Are there other fallacies? Of course. Some common fallacies you may be familiar with include the slippery slope.

If we legalize same-sex marriage, then what's next? That's just a slippery slope to marrying your pets! Or if we legalize marijuana that's a slippery slope to heroin addiction. We may also "beg the question," which assumes that the answer to your argument is contained within the argument itself. The first amendment to the US Constitution guarantees freedom of speech, so banning books is unlawful. Post hoc fallacies confuse correlation with causation. Just because X occurred before Y, does not mean that X caused Y. I went out to get my mail and it started raining. Guess I won't get my mail again unless I want it to rain.

## OTHER DISINFORMATION TACTICS

In addition to fallacies, disinformationists use other tactics to mislead. I get quite cranky when I see certain things that I know are intentionally misleading.

### Headlines

Headlines are some of my favorites to get me riled. I regularly read several newspapers each day, and I start with the headlines. Like many people, the more salacious the headline, the better. It will draw me in. What sometimes happens, though, is that the headline is salacious but has nothing at all to do with the article—a false connection.

Many people scan headlines in a newspaper or online to determine if they are going to read further. I am guilty as well. I have limited time and know my interests, so I am going to choose those articles that I will find interesting and that won't be a waste of time. Writers know this so they craft headlines to draw you in. That's the job of the headline. But the headline should also recap or summarize the gist of the article.

### Photos and Videos

Any misleading content, including misleading headlines, is problematic. What about content that is either manipulated, misleading, or just made up? It can be very easy to alter photos and videos. Heck, you can now create photos and videos using artificial intelligence. That makes it much more difficult to discern what is real from what is not. We have heard the term "fake news" used to discredit so-called "mainstream media" and sow doubt in the minds of people who are already distrustful of media. Misleading content may be considered legitimate "fake news."

Often, we see people use photos or videos out of context to "prove" a point. At the height of the Covid-19 pandemic, we saw many photos and videos used completely out of context. One of the more popular and egregious shows body bags stacked up allegedly in a New York City hospital. The photo and video are real, but they are not of bodies in a New York City hospital. They are of a hospital in Ecuador. This image certainly appealed to people's fears. Holy cow, we have all these people dead from Covid-19 just lying about in a hospital in New York City? Yikes!

Luckily several fact-checking organizations including the News Literacy Project debunked this video and photos. They did that via a reverse image search in Google. Google allows you to take an image and feed it into its search engine to determine the source of the image. Further, fact checkers were able to cull through the video to see posted signs that were consistent with photos from the hospital in question in Ecuador. Those signs were also in Spanish. With the growing interest in and use of artificial intelligence, it may be more difficult to tell real from fake. Fabricated content may be more prevalent. I will delve further into fact checking in Chapter 4.

## Numbers and Stats

What about numbers and statistics used incorrectly? I work with students who study communication. They are generally fearful of numbers and statistics. I am sure they are not in the minority. Statistics can be difficult to understand. We already discussed what happens when we don't understand something—we need to fill that information void. I often see this in the context of trend data or small numbers. A trend is a noticeable change over time. I would not say something is a trend if I have a week's worth of information. Not even a year. I want to see at least a decade or more to be able to make any sort of definitive comments. Sometimes people will say "it's trending down," with just a few months' worth of data. I guess, but that's hardly a trend. I also enjoy seeing people say things like, "25 percent of the folks in our group have left us" when you had just four people to begin with. (So, one person left?) Yes, you can perform statistical analysis on nearly anything, but does it make sense? Look at the entire picture. Words, context, and phrasing matter.

## Sponsored Content

Sponsored content is often spotted in magazines or newspapers. It looks like editorial content you might see in your regular publication. There may be a small disclaimer at the top or bottom that reads "sponsored content" or something similar. It is paid advertising. Sponsored content in this context refers to advertising and/or public relations disguising content as legitimate editorial content. I would also argue that "sponsored content" could be a research study, like one examining the effects of dairy on infant growth that was financially supported by the Dairy Council of the Americas. Such a study would be a clear conflict of interest disguised as research. Sponsored content may also include social media influencers who are given something to review or try. They may also be paid to say something good about a product. They should disclose that, but may not.

## Redirected Sites

When you visit a website, are you sure you have a legitimate website? Did you visit datadoyenne.com or did you visit thedatadoyenne.com? (The former is my actual website; the latter doesn't exist as of this writing.) What's the difference? Could be a lot. What if you are looking for CNN? The web address is CNN.com. If you type CNNNews.com you may be directed to a different site altogether. It may look and feel like CNN, but it is not. This is imposter content. Look at X (formerly known as Twitter). Who knows who you are viewing on that platform. Be careful of sites that seem to be other sites. Generally speaking—and I mean *generally* speaking—.org, .gov, and .edu sites are reputable. That said, there are no guidelines of use so anyone can start a .org site. Be careful.

## Propaganda

Propaganda is content that is used to persuade and change behaviors and attitudes. How does that differ from public relations and advertising? Some argue that it doesn't. Propaganda has a negative connotation, though, in that it is often untrue information, whereas advertising and public relations adhere to a code of ethics (believe it or not) and are truthful.

## Errors

Errors happen. How a news organization or other entity responds to errors is key. Do they issue a retraction? Retractions are never front and center. They are usually a small "article" in the paper. That said, most errors are not errors of fact but are attribution errors, spelling errors, date/time errors. They are not often huge errors that impact the meat and potatoes of a story.

## Misdirected Context

Context matters, particularly false context. I recently saw a conspiracy theory rear its ugly head. This conspiracy has been around as long as I've been alive (literally, it started in 1969, the year I was born). The theory is that the moon landing never happened. It is making the rounds on social media because Buzz Aldrin came out and said that he never landed on the moon. It didn't happen. But . . .

Evidently, Mr. Aldrin was on Conan O'Brien's show, *Conan*, in 2016. Mr. O'Brien said that he watched Mr. Aldrin land on the moon. Mr. Aldrin corrected him and said what he watched was a simulation/animation. Conspiracy theorists took that to mean that Mr. Aldrin didn't land on the moon. It played into the theory that the moon landing was faked. In fact, Mr. Aldrin clarified and said that no one recorded him stepping on the moon because...no one was there to video record it.

Neither Mr. Aldrin nor the other astronauts on the mission had the ability to capture this historic event on video. There is, however, an incredibly famous photo of Mr. Aldrin walking on the moon taken by Neil Armstrong. (If you zoom in you can see the reflection of someone taking the photo with the ship in the background.) Media outlets also were unable to get to the moon ahead of the landing to set up cameras to capture the event. (Of course, if they were able to do that, Mr. Armstrong wouldn't have been the first to walk on the moon, but I digress.) That doesn't mean it didn't happen.

Did you see the date of the Conan O'Brien episode? When something is reported or studied does matter. Think about this, though. This was a clip from a talk show from 2016. That's eight years ago. That's ancient! Yet it resurfaced. If you think that something that might be trending today can't come back once something new pops up, think again. Gah! We can't win the war on disinformation under such circumstance, but we will keep trying.

What does this have to do with context? If you take what Mr. Aldrin said without looking into the context of how it was said or why, you might assume that he is saying the moon landing was faked. However, watch the entire clip and you will see it differently. Don't rush to judgment without doing some research. If it seems suspect, it likely is.

During the Covid-19 pandemic, a humanities professor at a midwestern university recorded a Zoom lecture for his students for the first day of class. The video was intended to be humorous and, as he said, "to get the juices flowing." If you take some of his comments out of the video without watching/listening to the video, you might think this man should be fired. Calling students "vectors of disease," and noting that he assigns grades before the class starts were two comments. When I first saw the comments out of context, I thought, Holy cow! What is going on here? Then I watched the video. It's quite hilarious. It was not intended to offend. He was suspended as a result.

Something I worry about as a professor is a student taking something I've said out of context. That might happen if someone were to take just a snippet of my lesson or conversation and circulate it on social media without giving the context or the entire story. An example? I teach a course on crisis communication. Often, I will give the students a "crisis" to work on. That crisis is often something that could happen, but that is completely made up by me. Let's suppose they take that "crisis" and share it. If they don't note that it's taken out of context or made up, someone (or many) may believe it.

**Possible crisis scenario:** "The mayor of our town was accused of extorting money from the firefighters' union."
**Class assignment:** Assess whether this is a crisis or a problem. Then tell me how you, as the mayor's public relations expert, would

address this issue. I might also say, suppose it is true and then suppose it isn't. How you respond may differ.

If all you saw was "The mayor of our town was accused of extorting money from the firefighters' union," you might get very upset if you live in this town and even more upset if you are a firefighter. If, however, you see that it is part of a class assignment, you might giggle.

Context.

I am seeing far too many examples of a rush to judgment and many of them are in academia. To be fair, it could be because I am in academia and pay close attention to these issues.

## Satire

Satirical sites exist that are intended to poke fun at pop culture or important topics of the day. Such satire may be mistaken for legitimate news. Remember my reference to furries earlier? That started as satire. Birds Aren't Real is a satirical social movement spreading the idea that birds don't really exist but are rather drones created by the US government to spy on us. It was "created" in answer to the QAnon conspiracy theory as a lark (pun intended).

We might also consider satire and conspiracy theories hoaxes. I dedicate Chapter 8 to a discussion of conspiracy theories.

## ILLUSTRATING DISINFORMATION FALLACIES AND TACTICS

Let me use a couple of examples that may help to illustrate the above logical fallacies and other tactics. This will also highlight how they often overlap. One tactic may be present but often several rear their ugly heads.

"Trudeau and Biden wage arm wrestling competition to settle lunch money dispute." Perhaps that's the headline. I suspect that would draw many people in to read the article and even look at pictures or videos. Perhaps there is a picture of Biden rolling up his sleeves on a recent visit to Canada. That said, the article details a meeting between the two to try to figure out how the US might help Canada with the 2023 rash of wildfires.

He is rolling up his sleeves because he's warm. The phrase "lunch money" may be a slang term in Canada for something that is "easy" (if it isn't, I think it should be and this book might make it happen). Biden thinks solving the wildfire issue is easy; Trudeau does not. This is why they need to arm wrestle.

The example I used seems extreme and I hope it made you giggle. That said, it's not so far-fetched. Haven't we seen stories that have made us wonder if they are true because they seem so outside the norm, yet turn out to be true?

Of the various types of disinformation, which did I violate with my made-up story?

- **False connections.** The headline most definitely did not correspond to the content of the story.
- **Manipulated content.** I noted there was a photo of Biden rolling up his sleeves. The photo may be real, but it is being used to suggest he is getting ready for the arm-wrestling competition.
- **Misleading content.** The headline and the photo both mislead us. There is no grudge match, yet both lead us to believe we should buy tickets to a fight.
- **False context.** The content is genuine. The two men were meeting to discuss wildfires. There is no fight.
- **Error.** Perhaps this was done unintentionally by the news organization. Do we give them the benefit of the doubt? Perhaps.

In one short story with a photo and a headline, we see numerous tactics to deceive us. What about the other types of disinformation? Can I craft a story to describe them? Challenge accepted.

"Furries have invaded our high schools and now custodial staff must scramble to supply litter boxes in the hallways for those students who identify as cats."

That story was making its way around the internet. How did it start? It started as satire. There is a subculture of folks who dress up as animal characters. The idea that school-age children are doing so and requiring litter boxes was a complete hoax. This is an example of satire that was taken to be real. Sometimes it may be difficult to tell, but if something makes you say, huh? Go with that. Think about it. When you were in high school you probably didn't want to go to the bathroom at all let alone go in a litter box.

## WARNING SIGNS TO WATCH

In addition to the types of disinformation noted above, what are some other warning signs you should look for? If you see any of the following phrases, proceed with caution:

- **"Let that sink in."** This is really trying to get you to stop and think. It makes it seem as though you are getting some sort of information that requires you to think, perhaps do your own research and challenge established beliefs.
- **"The media won't report this."** I know there is great distrust of the media. Research studies bear this out. I can guarantee that the media is going to cover most things that are newsworthy. If you are getting this sort of supposed "insider information," media somewhere will report it. And I should stress that legitimate media will report it. You won't likely have information they don't or won't soon. Think about it. Do you really think if something big was going on that CNN or the BBC wouldn't cover it, but Bubba in his basement or Bob the Empire News Potato has the deets?
- **"Make this go viral or share this immediately with everyone you know."** Or some derivation of those three statements. This is a scare tactic to get you to act so that you may have a sort of "savior" complex. I knew all of this that the media won't cover and I must share. I am responsible for sharing it! I must let my community know! I will save the world!
- **"Do your own research."** Normally I am in favor of people doing their own research. But if someone says that in a post, be suspicious. If I am sharing information, I am not going to tell you to do your own research. I will have done the research and am reporting it to you. You can trust me. (If someone says, "trust me," run, run very fast.)

- **"There are no coincidences."** Actually, there are. This is another tactic to scare you into thinking that, of course, this must be true because, what are the odds? What are the chances?

How might this be presented? What if you see a post like the following: (Please note the following post is completely untrue—I made it up. Please also note that you aren't likely to see all the tropes noted above in one post.)

*OMG! Watermelons are not local, and the seeds are actually tiny microchips to track all your movements and manage your thoughts. They are grown by a coven of witches in Mexico who are trying to infiltrate the government and our churches. Let that sink in! My mother got one of these watermelons and now she sees drones outside her house all the time and she speaks in tongues. There are no coincidences! The media won't report this! It's too juicy! I mean, do your own research, but share this with everyone you know ASAP!*

Did you notice my pun? Is it too juicy? (I know, I know.) Also, the number of !!!! (exclamation marks). Everything is important! That's another giveaway.

Disinformation comes packaged in a number of costumes and disguises. These are just a few. It can be daunting to separate fact from fiction but it's not impossible.

# How Do You Know Something Is Disinformation?

**RECENTLY, I ASKED STUDENTS** in class to share a really bad data visualization. One student shared a graph from a source that cited data from the US Centers for Disease Control and Prevention (CDC). The data sounded and looked suspect to me, so I went to the CDC website to find the data referenced. Not there. Completely made up. Here was a guy creating visuals and accompanying explanation for his website. A man who has an online following sharing "data" from a credible source. Data that doesn't exist. But he said it came from the CDC. Due diligence is required. If something seems suspect, check it out. Don't accept everything at face value.

In this chapter, I will give you some tips to help you identify disinformation. You will be a hit at parties.

## KNOWING WHAT IS TRUE

How do we know if something is true or not? We can't just rely on feelings or instinct. We need more tangible ways to measure truthfulness and accuracy. Many sources and resources exist to help, but one of the best is the UC Berkeley Library.[10] I reference it here and break it down as follows:

- **Authority.** Who is the author? Is it someone you can trust?
- **Purpose.** Who is the intended audience for the piece? Why was it created?
- **Publication and format.** Where was it published? On social media? On a personal blog? In the newspaper?
- **Relevance.** Is it relevant to the topic? What is the scope?
- **Date of publication.** There are certainly seminal works that all researchers still reference (I am a huge proponent of Diffusion of Innovations—a theory formulated mid-last century, for example), but, generally, the more recent, the better.
- **Documentation**. Are sources cited? Who did they cite?

I'm going to unpack each of these more and really dig into how to assess what we read, hear, and see.

### Authority

Let's start with authority. The following is taken directly from the UC Berkeley Library website to describe what we should look for:

- Who is the author?
- What else has the author written?
- In which communities and contexts does the author have expertise?
- Does the author represent a particular set of world views?
- Do they represent specific gender, sexual, racial, political, social and/or cultural orientations?
- Do they privilege some sources of authority over others?
- Do they have a formal role in a particular institution (e.g., a professor at Oxford)?

Authority is who wrote the piece, who references the piece, and who is giving it voice in one way or another. For example, I consider myself an authority on several topics including infodemics. I have the credentials to back that up. I studied conflict resolution. I participated in the World Health Organization's Infodemic Manager Training Program. I could go on, but I think you get the point: I have some clout.

I have a PhD. It's in communication. One of my degrees is in biology. I have some science street cred. I do not, however, have enough clout to go on about quantum physics, for example. I can spell "quantum physics" which is about what I know about it (and you can bet that I triple-checked how to spell "quantum physics" so as not to embarrass myself). I am also not going to yammer on about Plato or Aristotle. Here's what I know about them: They're dead dude philosophers.

In addition to checking a person's credentials you should also check that those credentials are relevant to the topic at hand. Let's go back to quantum physics. I would feel comfortable writing about this topic if I talked to someone in the know. I have a good friend who is a physics professor. I would reach out to him to ask for guidance, information, and resources. Then I would feel confident distilling that information for my audience. I might even circle back to him so that he may read what I had written to be sure I have no errors of fact. I would absolutely note my sources which I would have reviewed to ensure they are good. I would make sure I added as much credence to my statements as possible, mindful that this is not necessarily my area of expertise.

I want you to think about that when you look to someone for advice. Let's consider Covid-19. I value the opinion of physicians on this subject with this caveat: I value the opinion of a public health physician or an infectious disease specialist over, say, a podiatrist. A podiatrist could know much about diseases and vaccines, but this might not be the first medical person I would seek out as an authority on the subject. This person has some legitimate credentials, but are they in an area of expertise you need?

That leads to a brief conversation about trust. (See Chapter 5 for more on trust.) Whom do you trust? How do you know whom to trust? Why should you trust them? I referenced the Edelman Trust Barometer earlier. I will reference some key data points from its 2023 top ten trust recap here:

- Distrust is our default. "Nearly 6 in 10 say their default tendency is to distrust something until they see evidence it is trustworthy."
- Business is one of the most trusted institutions (61 percent of those surveyed trust business); government and the media are not. ("Nearly one out of every two respondents view government and media as divisive forces in society—48 percent and 46 percent, respectively.")
- "Concerns over fake news or false information being used as a weapon is now at an all-time high of 76 percent."

There are other points, but I want to focus on these specifically. We default to distrust. I'm not necessarily opposed to that. I don't want people to automatically trust something. I want people to question it. That said, there are some institutions and people I do trust without thinking about it. Conversely, there are those I don't right off the bat.

We have also been fed such a toxic narrative about "fake news" that we don't necessarily trust any news anymore. That does sadden me. I've worked with journalists for years. All the journalists I know are as above board as anyone. They are also committed to truth-telling and fact-finding. Are there those who don't do that? Of course. I think you will find those bad eggs in every discipline. It is hardly journalism specific. That said, certainly question something if you think it is suspect. Journalists aren't above "authority."

What about influence and influencers? We hear these terms quite often. (As an aside, "influencers" back in the day were called "spokespersons." Just sayin'.) Please keep in mind that many so-called influencers are paid to review a product or service or say good things about it. Many will acknowledge that; many won't. Many will say good things regardless because they got something free; many will be honest and give you an accurate review. Be careful with influencers. Treat them as you would anyone else and ask, "By what authority?" I often read about TikTok Challenges that encourage people to do stupid things. "Hey, break open that Tide Pod and suck it back real fast while tapping the beat to a Beatles song with your foot and it will act as an aphrodisiac! Good night, sirs!" (I just made that up—or at least I hope I did. Please don't anyone do this.)

Don't do stupid shit because someone "dared" you or you think it will make you TikTok famous or something. Think before you act.

The problem with some of these so-called challenges and influencers is that they often have incredible reach. Many people follow them or share the challenges for any number of reasons. Remember Nicki Minaj? It may make the challenge or the influencer appear more popular than they are. Please don't equate "popularity" with "credibility" or "accuracy." Not. The. Same.

Remember, also, from Chapter 2 our conversation about trusted scientific sources and peer review. Make sure you consider that when looking at an authority.

Let me share another example. I know who the experts are, and I know how to take the information they need and want to share and make it palatable for the average person. I also know enough about science and health (I do have a BS in biology and have worked in health care for ages) to understand what is being said and what needs to be said.

I work with a colleague who is ridiculously intelligent. (To be fair, I work with many colleagues who are ridiculously intelligent.) Dr. Xiao-Ning Zhang is a biochemist and also a friend. I trust her. I've collaborated with her to help people understand Covid-19, vaccine efficacy, and safety. When I was approached by another colleague and friend, Dr. Rich Lee, about a hybrid journalism project for the Jandoli Institute that allowed communication/journalism professionals to collaborate with colleagues in other disciplines, I reached out to Xiao-Ning immediately. The idea was to work with a colleague to write a journalistic article so that they could understand how journalists work, but also so you could learn about other professionals and professions.

Cooperation and collaboration.

I wanted to write about Covid-19. She had other ideas. Since we have both done work for our county health department—and I still do work with them—she wanted to take some of the publicly available data and share with others how it might be used. I am familiar with much of the available data, but there is so much out there! Most people, I must believe, have no idea about the available data and if they do, they don't know what to do with it. We thought it would be wonderful to share with others why the data are important, how data may be used, and what the data mean.

I consider myself an authority in interpreting and communicating data. I consider Xiao-Ning an authority in this area also, but she has the additional content authority. She knows exactly what the data reference from a biologic/medical perspective. Our final article, "What Data Can Tell Us About the State of Health in Cattaraugus County," delves into the data to determine what our priorities should be as a county health department. Data are a driving strategy, as it should be.

What did we learn along the way? Xiao-Ning and I knew each other quite well, so I wouldn't say we learned anything earth shattering. We both agreed that the project reinforced for us the need to make sure we have accurate information and that we communicate it in a way that others will understand. Xiao-Ning noted that she writes in a very scientific way—which would be expected. She called my writing more "bubbly." Know your audience.

The best compliment she could have given me, though, was to say that I don't assume anything. I had questions about my interpretation of some data points and asked her if my explanation was correct. Did the way I worded and phrased something represent the facts? She liked that attention to detail because it mirrored her own in the way she approaches her research. Our fields aren't so different in terms of attention to detail.

In our current climate (and I would argue in any climate), getting something wrong is deadly—literally and figuratively. How often have you heard someone say, "Hey, they were wrong that one time, therefore, they are never right," or something like that? We all make mistakes. Do we own them and make corrections? Do we try our best to get it right at the outset? I usually hear comments like this related to the media. The media does issue corrections. Often, these corrections happen because of a misspelled name or wrong title. They aren't because the bulk of a story is inaccurate. Journalists are pilloried for these errors. I also see it in health care. When a health care professional makes a mistake, there is hell to pay. One might argue that when health care professionals make mistakes it could literally be deadly. Agreed. But please remember we are all human and capable of error. Have you never made an error while doing your job? If you say you never have, you are lying and we can't be friends.

Self-awareness is key. I know what I don't know. I might say I am an authority regarding what I don't know. I do know, however, who to reach out to get the right information. I know who I trust, and I know who the authority figures are. If you rattled off a list of categories or topic areas and asked me to give a name of someone I would contact to get information about that area, I would be ready to do that. Our collaborations and networks help to keep us honest. Working with others who are like us but who also complement us is key. I enjoy working with Xiao-Ning and others because we have much in common, but we also have key differences. We bring something unique to the table that the other does not. It's a sci-comm symbiosis—like a lichen (if you have no idea what that means, look it up—lichen is pretty fascinating).

To recap: Authority is one element to consider when deciding if something is truthful or not. Trust is also important and helps to lend credibility to the authority. Influencers should be treated as you would any other authority.

## Purpose

Next let's tackle purpose. What is the purpose of:

- The article you've read (or are reading)?
- The study that was conducted?
- The picture/video you've seen/watched (or are seeing/watching)?
- The social media post you've seen and shared?

I refer again to UC Berkeley's Library resource to help you determine if something is legitimate. The following is taken directly from its site related to purpose:

- Why was this source created?
- Does it have an economic value for the author or publisher?
- Is it an educational resource? Persuasive? What (research) questions does it attempt to answer? Does it strive to be objective?

- Does it fill any other personal, professional, or societal needs?
- Who is the intended audience?
- Is it for scholars?
- Is it for a general audience?

Let's look at a few examples.

It may be obvious who the intended audience is just by noting the tone or the subject matter. For example, advertising for weight-loss programs like WW are clearly targeted to those of us who are overweight or struggle with weight, primarily women. (We can argue whether we should be promoting a "healthy body type," but that's a separate issue.) It is quite clear from the messaging that it understands its audience. That is the first rule in any communication campaign. Understand your audience. I pick on Weight Watchers (WW) because I have had success with its program. I also think it provides a ready example of the intended audience coupled with appropriate messaging.

The messaging does have economic benefit for the WW corporation. It may also be considered educational and certainly persuasive. It also fills a personal need. Is it objective? You decide.

Here's another example. In 2016, the *Canadian Medical Association Journal* reported on studies "conducted" by the Dairy Research Cluster.[11] It sounds legit, right? A group of scientists looking at the efficacy of dairy products. What's the problem?

The Dairy Research Cluster consisted of Agriculture and Agri-Food Canada (contributing more than $13 million), "Dairy Farmers of Canada ($5.3 million), the Canadian Dairy Network ($669,000) and the Canadian Dairy Commission ($750,000)." The point? To "promote the efficiency and sustainability of Canadian dairy farms, grow markets, and supply high-quality, safe and nutritious dairy products to Canadians."

Um, what? Research funded by the people it would benefit? I mentioned this in the last chapter in reference to sponsored content. It happens more than I would like. Legitimate scientists were working on research funded by this Cluster, but one must wonder how unbiased it can be when it is funded by those who would most directly benefit. What happens if the scientists find that dairy is harmful and should not be part of a healthy diet? Do they get put out to pasture? (I said puns are always intended.)

Moo-ving right along (I can't help myself!) with one more example.

Much has been written about the anti-vaccination movement. In fact, the movement has a wonderful moniker—the Disinformation Dozen. About twelve different players are responsible for about 73 percent of the vaccine disinformation on Facebook, and 17 percent of posts on X (Twitter) according to a report from the Center for Countering Digital Hate.[12] If you look at one of the most prolific—Robert F. Kennedy Jr.'s Children's Health Defense—you will see a very professional-looking website. Who is this site for? One might assume it's for anyone who is against vaccines or is anti-vax curious. Digging a bit, it is clear to me that he is targeting mothers of children. In fact, the team and board of directors have not one physician. There are two attorneys and several people who are life-long advocates. Most are women and mothers.

And why do I say it targets women and mothers? Its title is Children's Health Defense. Having worked in health care I can tell you that often health care marketing is targeted to women because generally men don't manage the health care of anyone in the family, including themselves (no offense to men who do but… statistics).

Why was this "source" (the website and organization) created? The site has a .org URL ending, which is one I often say may have legitimate information on it (not always and, remember, others may be .gov and .edu). Was it created for some monetary gain? Perhaps, but more importantly, it was created to be persuasive. It purports to be an educational resource. There are many articles, videos, interviews, etc., that a site visitor may reference to educate herself (again, primarily for women) about the dangers of vaccines. Do your own research!

It has a name many recognize: Kennedy. Many may also associate that name with credibility. Does it strive to be objective? I will let you decide.

If you do look at the website, consider the tactics used to share information. Look at the social media associated with the site. The site itself is very well put together. It is professional. It looks legitimate. (To be fair, they believe their information to be accurate and legitimate.) Disinformationists know what to do to persuade.

## Publication and Format

The publication and/or format of the source of information is also important. I read everything—or nearly so. Magazines? Yes (my former mail carrier used to call me the Magazine Lady—could be worse monikers, I suppose). Newspapers? Three a day. Books? If only I had more time to read more books!

What specifically do I read? I read international/national, regional, and local newspapers. I need to know what's going on. Magazines? What don't I read! I am sad that several of my favorite magazines are either no longer published or are available as online versions only. My favorite? *National Geographic*. Gotta keep my nerd cred.

Academic journals? Lately I've found myself looking for research on infodemics. You may or may not be surprised to know that you can find all sorts of research on this topic—or variations of this topic—in many journals. I like the fact that it has interdisciplinary attention.

Why do I go into this detail?

The publications you read or get your information from matter. The format may also matter. I tend to find reputable publications. How do I know? Oh, recall my reiteration of the things to consider when evaluating materials (continued shout out to the Library at UC Berkeley). The following regarding publication and format is taken from its site:

- Where was it published?
- Was it published in a scholarly publication, such as an academic journal?
- Who was the publisher? Was it a university press?
- Was it formally peer-reviewed?
- Does the publication have a particular editorial position?
- Is it generally thought to be a conservative or progressive outlet?
- Is the publication sponsored by any other companies or organizations? Do the sponsors have biases?
- Were there any apparent barriers to publication?
- Was it self-published?
- Were there outside editors or reviewers?

- Where, geographically, was it originally published, and in what language?
- In what medium?
- Was it published online or in print? Both?
- Is it a blog post? A YouTube video? A TV episode? An article from a print magazine?
- What does the medium tell you about the intended audience?
- What does the medium tell you about the purpose of the piece?

Whew. That seems like a lot to consider. You just want to read something or watch something. You don't want to think! Many of the considerations above relate to other areas we've already discussed like Authority and Purpose. Let's unpack things a bit more.

Let's suppose that I Google "incidents of voter fraud in the US." (I have not done this, so the following is completely made up by me to show as an example.) Say I am concerned about voter fraud because elections are coming up; I am an election-poll worker; I am a concerned citizen; I don't want democracy to die while I am alive. (When I'm dead, all bets are off.)

Let's suppose I see a piece from CNN (a rather reputable news outlet that tends to lean left). I see another piece from Pew Research (a very reputable research organization that is about as unbiased as you are going to get). I also see a blog post from someone calling himself Dr. Phil Ballott. I've heard of CNN and Pew Research. In fact, I often cite Pew Research and have done so in this book. I will look at this post, but I am also interested in Dr. Ballott. I've never heard of him yet he is showing up in the search. What does he have to say?

The post leads to a rather well-organized website with a picture of a stereotypical academic (mussed hair, goatee, blazer with suede elbow patches, all taken in front of a messy shelf of books—hey, I know my stereotypes). His bio indicates that he is a political science professor from Stanford University. His bio states that he has done work at Pew Research (extra points for Phil). His site is dedicated to educating the public about the dangers of our voting system in America. He and his team of graduate students have studied this extensively and are here to report what the media won't tell you! (Red flag.) He has several blog posts on the topic.

He has not one post that is academic, though. No references to academic journal articles and no references to any studies he has conducted or interviews he may have done with major media organizations. Looking at his social media outlets, it looks like he has 100K followers on X (Twitter) and another 50K on Facebook. Wow, he has a community!

I am fascinated because Dr. Ballott seems legitimate.

Or does he?

In case you aren't familiar with academia, that would be understandable because many academics live in this ivory tower that isn't easily explained even by them. (Yes, I'm an academic, but I'm a non-academic, academic.) If Dr. Ballott is a professor at Stanford or anywhere, I should be able to find him on the university's website, right? Of course I should. Hmmmm.... a search of Stanford's website doesn't show this guy at all. (Dear readers, I made this guy up. If one of you goes to Stanford's website and finds a Dr. Ballott working in the political science department, I will eat my shoe.) Stanford is an incredibly reputable institution. If this guy works there, he must have some research chops. He would tout that loudly on his website. Nope. Also, he would be searchable on Google and other academic-related pieces would show up. And I have yet to meet an academic who has that kind of social media following! (Now I'm just being mean.)

When I Google him what do I find? (Again, making this up for example's sake.) I find that some folks questioned his legitimacy and were commenting on it on Reddit. I look at the Reddit thread. I don't take everything I see on Reddit at face value, but it is often humorous and can lead you to other information that might be helpful.

I see that someone on the thread "exposed" Dr. Ballott. I do some further digging and find out that Dr. Phil Ballott is actually Chad Hanger from Florida. He is a conspiracy theorist who writes posts for this website from his parents' basement. He also likes nachos and Alex Jones (Facebook reveals much). Suddenly I don't care what Dr. Ballott has to say.

Sadly, he is posting, and others are reading it and they aren't paying attention to who he is or that he is lying. He is spreading disinformation for his own pleasure. He clearly has an itch to scratch (and if he's eating nachos in the basement, those crumbs might get pesky, and he might have a literal itch to scratch—I don't judge, except that I do).

You might think this is harmless but remember that he is appealing to many emotions here. People finding his untruths may also be worried about democracy and he may be playing to their fears. Perhaps there are others who feel as he does so he now has a community—and a sizable one judging from his social following.

Neither his website nor his social media posts are peer reviewed. You always hear peer review in the context of academic journals and research, but I argue that you see it in other areas like actual book publishing (not self-publishing), newspaper editorials, etc., as I've mentioned earlier. I can write a wonderful piece for *The New York Times* editorial page and the editors in charge might say, "Um, no, thanks for playing." They are my peers, and they are reviewing my work for acceptability and publication.

Dr. Phil Ballott also has a clear editorial slant. Generally speaking, generally speaking (it bears repeating), reputable outlets are unbiased. We can argue, and I have, that you can never truly be unbiased. Let me rephrase that statement then. Reputable outlets are as unbiased as is possible.

Dr. Ballott also used a phrase we are to be wary of, right? "The media won't report this!" Of course, the media is going to report something like this if it is legitimate. That just lends to the fear and appeals to the community of those who feel like media outsiders.

The example I used may be an easy one to unpack and may be obvious. The work I did to unpack it may seem arduous and it is. If you see something that seems too good to be true or seems suspect in any way, dig deeper. Scratch your own itch! Remember that publication and format are important considerations in determining the truthfulness of a piece.

## Relevance

Next, ask yourself if what you are reading or viewing or listening to relevant to the question at hand. What does UC Berkeley's Library resource have to say about relevance and documentation (taken directly from its website)?

- How is it relevant to your research?
- Does it analyze the primary sources that you're researching?

- Does it cover the authors or individuals that you're researching, but different primary texts?
- Can you apply the authors' frameworks of analysis to your own research?
- What is the scope of coverage?
- Is it a general overview or an in-depth analysis?
- Does the scope match your own information needs?
- Is the time period and geographic region relevant to your research?
- Did they cite their sources? If not, do you have any other means to verify the reliability of their claims?
- Who do they cite?
- Is the author affiliated with any of the authors they're citing?
- Are the cited authors part of a particular academic movement or school of thought?
- Did they appropriately represent the context of their cited sources?
- Did they ignore any important elements from their cited sources?
- Are they cherry-picking facts to support their own arguments?
- Did they appropriately cite ideas that were not their own?

You may be reading the above and thinking, "I'm not doing this kind of research, so how do I translate this for my own use?" Challenge accepted. When thinking about whether something is relevant, you may consider its relevance to your "research," but more likely you will consider the scope of coverage.

Let's suppose we have an important election on the horizon. We have all seen campaign ads from different candidates. We are also seeing and hearing commentary and/or news stories about the problems of fraudulent elections. Also, as long as I can remember, we've heard about dead people voting. (It turns out dead people do not vote. They also don't do anything else like drink wine or go to the gym.)

What if you see a "report" that notes that voting by mail is rife with fraud. Let's unpack that. Who is doing the reporting? What evidence do they have? Who is reporting this evidence? Is the word of one person being relied on or is there a more in-depth analysis? Where is this alleged fraud?

Are we talking about South America or the US? Is the "side" alleging the fraud doing so in an area that is heavily weighted toward the other side? Those are things to consider.

Let's take another example. Winter occurs in many areas of the world. With winter comes an increased risk of Covid-19, flu, and other respiratory ailments. What if you see a report that those who are unvaccinated are at greater risk of contracting respiratory ailments? You and those you care about are vaccinated. Is that information relevant to you? It may certainly be an in-depth analysis, but does it match your current information needs? We could argue that it is the responsibility of all of us to ensure our community is safe so we should care about all members, but we can only do what we can do. Unlike my voting example, the respiratory ailment scenario is true. Those who are unvaccinated are at greater risk. Even if we work with accurate information, we may still assess whether it is relevant to us and whether we need to take some action. Now, if you have a family member who is opposed to vaccines, this may be a bit different (Chapter 9 deals with having conversations with those who believe disinformation).

Let's use our two scenarios to look at documentation. "Voting by mail is rampant and fraudulent." We noted what was relevant information, but let's look at the documentation you may see surrounding it. What sources are cited in this reporting? Again, is it just one person or are there many? Are those people able to truly know that absentee voting is fraudulent? Are people who would have that information cited or not? Is information being cherry picked to suit the story? (Reminder…there is no evidence whatsoever that voting by mail in the US is fraudulent.)

What about respiratory ailments? When you read reports like this you are—or should be—hearing from epidemiologists, infectious disease specialists, medical doctors, and public health practitioners. In other words, specialists who know! One might argue, "Well, what about the other side? Shouldn't we listen to those who are opposed to vaccines?" Well, sure if you are going to unpack that information in the same way. Documentation is all about citations and giving credit where credit is due. It is also about citing documentation and sources that are relevant, timely, expert, accurate, and purposeful.

## Date of Publication

Next in our "how do we know it's legit" puzzle is Date of Publication. What does UC Berkeley's Library resource have to say about date of publication? When exploring this, ask:

- When was the source first published?
- What version or edition of the source are you consulting?
- Are there differences in editions, such as new introductions or footnotes?
- If the publication is online, when was it last updated?
- What has changed in your field of study since the publication date?
- Are there any published reviews, responses, or rebuttals?

Why does this matter? Oh, it matters a great deal. Let's talk.

One of the things I often say to students is that it is difficult to find a textbook that works for a class about anything related to social media (I have managed to find some good ones, though). Why is that? The length of time it takes to write a textbook, find a publisher, get it published, develop the associated materials for the book, and distribute it/sell it, could be a couple of years or more. Social media changes every ten minutes (I exaggerate, but not by much). How do you keep a book like this up to date? With e-books, it is a bit easier. Updates may be made more easily and quickly.

One may argue that the strategies behind the use of social media don't change. You still need to know what the purpose of your plan is and where social media fits in. Learning about specific social media tools is something you just need to figure out. Yes, and...it sounds like you are talking a bit about an evolution of sorts.

We've already talked about the Scientific Method and how it works. Remember that science is an evolution. It is a process that is constantly in motion. It is one person or team of people working to increase our understanding of the world. Sometimes things change. Certainty is an illusion.

Do you remember late 2019/early 2020? I think we all do. What did we know about Covid-19? We knew that it was a virus originating in Wuhan, China, that spread rapidly. We didn't completely know how it was transmitted. If you recall the early days, we were told to wear masks to safeguard ourselves and others. This is certainly wise advice to prevent any sort of spread of an airborne disease. I also recall that people would have groceries delivered but would keep them outside for a period or would wipe everything off, including the mail. We weren't quite sure if the virus could live on solid surfaces and for how long. We also didn't know how it might impact certain groups of people. We did learn that those who were older and/or those with comorbidities didn't fare as well and may have been more susceptible to dying.

Then there is long Covid. We are still understanding the impact of it.

Some of the confusion may have been in not knowing what we were dealing with at first but also in thinking we were dealing with something we'd seen before. Covid-19 is a respiratory infection that presents as pneumonia-like. It was treated as such at first, but it was found that treatments for pneumonia didn't work against Covid-19. The rush to a vaccine was on! Enter mRNA vaccines. Then recall the conversation about the rush to vaccine creation. Remember, with Covid-19, we were seeing the scientific method in action—the wizard behind the curtain.

The timeline was rapid. The world shut down. Then the finger-pointing began. I recall hearing people say, "You told us we had to wipe everything down and now we don't have to." That's right, but isn't a clean house nice? We took precautions because we didn't have all the information. We were asked to do things based on past experience with similar viruses before we knew we weren't really dealing with a similar virus—or not similar enough.

Many people were worried because it seemed that the vaccines came to market quickly. Remember, though, that scientists have been working with and studying vaccines for decades. They understand how they work even if they may not have completely understood the disease they were working with.

Confusion over the nature of Covid-19 and the seeming rush to market of the vaccine led to widespread disinformation that spread as quickly as Covid-19 itself! Think about the rumors and outright untruths associated with the virus. A plot by China to stop the world's economy. A plot by democrats in the US to prevent the reelection of President Trump. An overreaction to the flu. I could go on.

If we go back to 2020 and read some of the news reports or journal articles about Covid-19, we would have a very different picture of the disease than reading an article from 2022. Time matters. Think about that when you encounter a story or seek information. When was the report you are reading first published? Has it been updated? Have other reputable sources commented on it and adjusted? Have there been additional studies that add to that research or that debunk it?

Are there seminal studies we still look to that are old? Sure. I often reference Diffusion of Innovations in my classes and other work including in this book (which you read about earlier). It is a theory posited in 1962. That's old by research standards. It still holds up, though. Have others done research in this area? Absolutely they have but, to my knowledge, no one has changed the theory. We still talk about innovators, early adopters, etc. We still reference opinion leaders. We still reference Everett Rogers. Several of the theories and ideas I present in this book are based on seminal studies and works that have stood the test of time and are not "recent."

## Documentation and Sources

In addition to authority, purpose, publication and format, relevance, date and documentation, also consider source, headlines, supporting evidence, biases, and fact-checkers.

When considering the source, you want to look at the author but also where it appeared or from where. Where did they get it? Recall the example of Buzz Aldrin and his alleged discounting of the moon landing. Who shared that information and with whom? Why? Always read behind the headlines as I noted earlier. They can be deceiving. Does the piece you are looking at provide any supporting evidence? Is it just making claims? Furries need litter boxes in high schools! Based on what information? (As an aside, I did have someone tell me that our local school had litter boxes. I know the school board president and asked her if it was true. She asked if I'd been drinking at work.) Is there evidence—and relevant, accurate evidence?

## CHECK YOUR BIASES... AND YOUR SOURCES

What about your own biases? We all have them. In addition to what I've noted in this chapter so far, let's talk about how we identify some less-obvious or difficult-to-discern information. We may certainly use the above tactics to determine disinformation in several forms from the written word to photos to videos to artificial intelligence. That later may be more difficult to scrutinize.

In Chapter 2, I mentioned a photo that was widely shared during the pandemic. I also gave some information about using Google's reverse image search feature to find out when and where that image first appeared. Google and other sites have several features that may help you look at photos and videos to determine their legitimacy. I also encourage you to take a look at the News Literacy Project site. Both Google and NewsLit.org have lessons that you may take yourself or share with others that help you maneuver through the mayhem. I will give a more complete list in Chapter 10, as well as on my website.

The Union of Concerned Scientists[13] suggests you ask yourself the following questions when you see something that might be suspect:

- Is it difficult to separate facts from opinions?
- Does it fail to cite experts from reputable organizations?
- Is the original source of the information hard to pin down?
- Does it confirm your beliefs, or play to your emotions?
- Does the group, person, or organization sharing the information have a stake in the claim (financial, political, or otherwise)?
- Does it require belief in a secret plot and a group of co-conspirators?
- Does it scapegoat people or groups?
- Is it spread by someone who recently started their social media account but has a lot of followers?

The Union of Concerned Scientists suggest we also look at when someone started their account. If you see that someone just created the account and they have thousands of followers, be suspect. That is a red flag. No one gets that many followers right away unless they are a celebrity, I suppose.

What should you do if you see something that is disinformation? The first thing you should NOT do is share it! The News Literacy Project encourages #CareBeforeYouShare. Don't perpetuate the myth!

## Where Do People Get Their News?

I always ask my students where they get news. In my classroom, I am dealing with a small number of people, but they often represent the whole. Almost all of them said they get their news online. Keep in mind, I am teaching Gen Z. My first thought is, **No!** Then I ask where they go online. I am heartened to hear that they get information from actual news sources, but they use the online apps or the news outlets social media feeds. Phew.

Where do others get news? Pew Research[14] released data in 2021 noting where people get news. About half of Americans get their news on social media with Facebook, YouTube, X (Twitter), and Instagram topping the list. More women than men get news from Facebook, while white men, particularly, get news from Facebook and Reddit. Black and Hispanic adults rely on Instagram. Those differences also vary by age. Younger people rely on TikTok, Snapchat, Reddit, Instagram, and X more than other social media sites. Those with a college education rely on LinkedIn, Reddit and X. Sadly, another Pew Research study noted that those who rely on social media for their news are less knowledgeable about politics.[15] They are also more likely to see and hear false claims and conspiracy theories. Specifically, those who rely on social media have seen and heard two false claims related to Covid-19: Vitamin C prevents Covid-19 and the connection between 5G and the virus. Americans who get their news from social media are more apt to believe that Covid-19 originated in a lab.

Government officials and others have tried to ban or legislate that social media sites manage the level of disinformation found on the sites. Recent studies, though, show that it may not help because the impact of disinformation found on social media sites may not be what it was initially thought. A study by Brendan Nyhan, et al, published in July 2023 showed that people are seeing content online from others like them most of the time, with political and news information a small portion of that.[16] Reducing the number of exposures during the 2020 US presidential election cycle didn't change people's beliefs or attitudes.

Algorithms are always in question when it comes to social media. If you think about the content you see on social media platforms, it's likely information or news or entertainment that you want to see. It is content that you prefer. The algorithms may change periodically, but suffice to say, the platforms are giving you what you allegedly want.

Finally, I do want to say a bit about the old adage, "There are two sides to every story." That may be true. There may be three sides. There may be just one. Often journalists are expected to cover both sides of a news story. Should they? Should we hear from the other side if the other side is not even close to accurate? An excellent example of this is a discussion of the Holocaust. I would argue there is one side to this story: genocide perpetrated by the Nazi regime in Germany. Are there Holocaust deniers? Yes. Do we need to provide them ink? No, we do not. There is no evidence that the Holocaust did not happen.

The Sandy Hook School shooting, sadly, happened. There are deniers. Do we need to provide them ink? No, we do not. With one exception—look for that in an upcoming chapter.

Keep in mind that people won't always take the necessary steps to determine if something is real. Why is that? I'll tackle that question in the next chapter.

# Trust No One

**TRUST.** I feel as though who we trust or what we trust has just completely broken down. I see this in words and actions. I see this in what I read in the paper or on social media and in what I hear people say and do—myself included. I started down the disinformation path to address our collective move away from science and reason and to help people understand how to find accurate information. I wanted to focus on how to trust what's out there and weed through the rhetoric of disinformation.

What is trust? Whether we can define trust or not, we probably each have an idea of what it is. We can think of specific examples such as the fact that I trust my sister to not listen to my podcast or read my blog (she admitted as much and it made me sad, but I understand). I trust that the vaccine and booster I've gotten will protect me from a serious case of Covid-19. I trust that the red wine I will drink later will turn me into Aristotle, Einstein, and Cindy Crawford. (Choose your own drunken manifestations.) You get the point.

In this chapter I will unpack trust and how important it is in understanding the sharing of disinformation. Who do we trust and why?

## TEST YOUR TRUST BAROMETER

The barometer of trust looks different for everyone. I trust certain news and other outlets. When I compile information, I turn to trusted sources of information. I reference Pew Research (I turn to it again and again). I also reference data from the Edelman Trust Barometer. Yes, Edelman is a public relations firm, and I know many people don't trust PR. I worked in PR for several years and still consider myself a practitioner. A few years ago, I had a friend—a friend—say to me that all PR is lies. She's dead now because I killed her. (That last part is untrue. I did not kill anyone, but I did school her in PR.) Are there some PR practitioners who are less than ethical? Sure. You could restate that question with any field/job and still get the same answer. Examples:

- Are there some doctors who are less than ethical? Sure.
- Are there some professors who are less than ethical? Sure.
- Are there some CEOs who are less than ethical? Sure.
- Are there some _____ who are less than ethical? Sure.

Note the use of the word "some." I did not write "all." There is a difference. It also doesn't mean we shouldn't trust.

Do you trust your professors or other academics? I hope so. Michigan State University notes that "people say that trust is the #1 characteristic they want in a partner, and trust is what makes human communities work."[17]

Noted researcher and educator Brené Brown offers the acronym **BRAVING** to discuss qualities that contribute to trust: Boundaries, Reliability, Accountability, Vault, Integrity, Non-judgement, and Generosity.[18]

- **Boundaries.** We must set boundaries in all relationships. Understand what that means.

- **Reliability.** Can I count on you? Do we do this ourselves? I often say yes to things and then realize I've screwed myself. I get it done but not as well as I would like.
- **Accountability.** Own your shit. People like it when you take the blame when you did something wrong.
- **Vault.** Do not share my secrets.
- **Integrity.** Courage over comfort. Doing what is right. Ethical guidelines.
- **Non-judgment.** I can lose my shit and you'll just pick me back up.
- **Generosity.** Assume my intentions—and yours—are good.

We can dissect this in the context of infodemics. Are the boundaries we establish part of an echo chamber? We may find others who feel as we do—the belonging—and establish a filter bubble around them and us. We rely on them to give us information to help fill any knowledge voids we have. We hold ourselves accountable just as they would. We also count on the group to keep secrets and to do what is right. We don't want to be judged—we have the rest of the world to do that. We assume we are all in this group for the same thing and to the same end. We will look out for one another.

We need to establish trust because we can't do it all. I have no interest whatsoever in doing my own taxes. Could I? I am sure I could figure it out, but I'm going to trust someone who actually studied this in school and passed a licensing exam. I would say that person is more qualified than me. When I formed an LLC for Data Doyenne, I could have gone online and figured out how to do that, but I contacted an attorney who specializes in this. I don't change the oil in my car. The person who does knows what he is doing so I let him.

## EXPLORING THE DATA ON TRUST

I've referenced the Edelman Trust Barometer previously. Why do I like it? This is a survey that is done each year and has been done for the past 21 years. It is an online survey. The most recent was done in twenty-eight countries with 33,000+ respondents. That sure isn't an N of 1. The Trust

Barometer measures trust in business, government, NGOs, and media.

We've noted that the most glaring change in the past year is the eroding trust in government—and that's worldwide. Anyone who watches or reads the news won't be surprised by that. Also included in this would be eroding trust in our global leaders. The Trust Barometer does note the top ten takeaways from the research. Number one? "Distrust is now society's default emotion."

Pew Research did its own study in 2019[19] (just ahead of the pandemic—keep that in mind). Note the similarities in the research. What I like about the Pew study is that it digs into the data to note demographic and psychographic differences in trust. Note that the Pew Research study is for the United Stated while the Edelman Trust Barometer is global.

I find some of the data particularly compelling. For example, our trust in government has eroded considerably. The Pew Research study notes that from 1958 to the present, trust in the US government has gone from a high of nearly 80 percent to about 20 percent in 2018. What?

In addition, Pew Research notes that interpersonal trust had also eroded. A 2018 study indicated that 71 percent of adults in the US believe we in the US are less confident in each other than we were two decades ago. What is the reason for the decline? Societal and policy problems topped the list at 43 percent, followed by government activity/inactivity (16 percent), technology/internet/social media (12 percent), problems with the news and media and information (11 percent). (That doesn't add up to 100 percent because I am reporting just the top choices and respondents were able to choose more than one.)

The same study also noted that 25 percent of adults believe Americans don't have confidence in one another. Why? A lack of trust related to societal problems was cited by 67 percent of respondents. We don't feel as though others will act responsibly and ethically. That lack of trust extends to our confidence that people will do the right thing when confronted with an ethical dilemma. We don't trust.

There are generational differences, too. Older Americans trust their neighbors and others to do the right thing more than young people do. For example, older Americans are more confident than younger Americans in believing that others will respect the rights of those who are not like them.

One might argue young people aren't cynical enough yet to have that opinion!

That's in the United States. What about trust globally? Our World in Data reported on a 2014 study assessing whether people can be trusted or not.[20] Many parts of the world did not agree with the statement "Most people can be trusted." Interestingly, the responses varied depending on how affluent a country was. The larger the gross domestic product (GDP), the more people agreed with the statement. Money may not buy happiness, but I guess it buys trust.

## WHY DO WE BELIEVE?

We each have our own biases. You might say, "Nope, not me. I'm super awesome." You may be, but you still have biases. I'm not saying you have racist or homophobic tendencies, but biases go beyond what may be used to discriminate. They certainly may be stereotypical responses to stimuli, but they usually go beyond that.

Why do people believe disinformation? Why do people believe anything? There are several explanations that may overlap in our understanding of why people believe as they do. Let's dissect them.

### Confirmation Bias

Let's talk about confirmation bias. This is the tendency we likely all have to seek out information that supports our beliefs. We may be faced with facts, data, and science, but we are still largely led by our beliefs and belief systems. That is not to say that we shouldn't hold fast to our beliefs, but we should also be open to other insights. If facts present themselves, take a look. There are many examples of confirmation bias. We often see confirmation bias when religion and science collide. Evolution provides a good example. There is ample scientific evidence to support the theory of evolution yet there are some who believe the world was created by God in six days despite evidence to the contrary. When presented with said evidence, those who staunchly believe that the world was created by God will seek out evidence (the Bible and fellow believers) to support their beliefs, science be damned.

Let's think about our own behaviors, and I will use myself as an example. If I listed for you the media I consume, you could make a number of assumptions about me and my beliefs. Do I seek out alternate viewpoints? Sometimes. Should I? Yes! Do you? Should you? If I type the phrase: "Are the Buffalo Bills better than the Buffalo Sabres?" (Can you guess where I'm from?) I might get search results that note that the Bills are better than the Sabres. If I reverse the statement to read: "Are the Buffalo Sabres better than the Buffalo Bills?" I may get the reverse. Our own search behaviors may impact the information we receive. Did you ever search for something online and then see it everywhere in your social media feeds? Algorithms show us what we like and what we want to see. That's helpful from an advertising point of view but not helpful if we are trying to counter confirmation bias. I mean, that's the reason I suggested searching atom before anus in Chapter 2 and the reason I don't search for porn online (I read *National Geographic* for its aboriginal porn).

## Cognitive Bias

Fear, anxiety, and emotion drive many of our actions. Cognitive bias exists when we can't easily explain something. We want simplification. We want easy. If something is difficult or mysterious, it can be frightening. We need to find an explanation. What does that mean? Like confirmation bias, we pay attention to information that confirms our beliefs. This may help when things are unexplained. We are also trying to find others like us. We all want to feel as though we belong, and seeking out those who believe as we do is one way to ensure community. We may also get a bit of information and assume we have all the information we need. We then make assumptions based on a little info because a little goes a long way, as they say. We also like to blame. Someone or something must be at fault, and that explanation should be easy. Information voids exist and disinformationists exploit those voids.

Let's look at Covid-19 again. We want to blame all of China for unleashing this disease Kraken. As a result, we have seen incidences of hate crimes against Asians and Asian-Americans increase. We are blaming an entire population of people who had nothing to do with the pandemic. We also want to really pinpoint the origin. Yes, it originated in China. Was it a lab (which would play into the conspiracy theory that China unleashed the virus willingly for its own gain) or was it our own human collective interactions with wild animals that allowed the virus to jump species? We may never know, but that doesn't stop people from proselytizing. It also returns us to the conversation about nomenclature. When people referred to Covid-19 as "the China virus" we didn't do ourselves any favors. It hearkened back to the Spanish Flu moniker. Words and names matter! With the Spanish Flu, scientists gave it that name because it was believed to have originated in Spain. The name was easy. Easy sometimes bites us in the ass.

## Partisan Bias

We have also seen partisan bias in the United States and elsewhere in the world. This occurs when we so fervently believe the ideologies and rhetoric of one party over another. Of course, confirmation and cognitive biases play a big role in this belief also. We want to belong. We believe many things a particular party may be saying so we jump on the bandwagon and sign on for everything.

## Echo Chambers

We also see post-truth which allows us to trust our emotions more than logic and reason. Echo chambers are similar to what we've already discussed. These are figurative "chambers" in which we find ourselves. We only hear, listen to, and see what confirms our biases and then seek continued validation. We hear an "echo" of what we already know and believe. Filter bubbles refer to the "bubble" you find yourself in based on online algorithms or groupthink. Filter bubbles are like echo chambers in that you are essentially recycling the same information over and over from the same and similar sources. You don't get anything new or different or challenging. If you do, you ignore it, don't click on it, scroll right by. That lack of engagement impacts your online algorithms.

## Simplification

Much disinformation also simplifies complex issues. We don't like to think any more than we have to. We want things given to us in as simple a way as possible. Disinformationists are gifted at creating information that does just that.

## HOW DISINFORMATIONISTS CAPITALIZE ON BIAS

Do you see common themes in what I presented? Why do disinformationists do such a good job? They know they need to:

- Appeal to your fears, emotions, and anxieties
- Simplify
- Create "community" (or make it seem like a community)

Let's unpack each of these.

### Appeals to Fear

I've mentioned them in different sections of this book, but let me expand on them here. We each have fears. It may be fear of the unknown; fear of change; fear of being alone. Then there are phobias which are irrational fears but fears nonetheless. When we are afraid, we want to not be afraid. This doesn't count watching a scary movie in which case you want to be afraid. In real life, we want to be in a position of less, rather than more fear. What do we do when we are afraid? Try to not be! This is something we got through evolution. Most animals when faced with a fearful situation, try to get out of it. That might be by running to escape being eaten, or by hiding to escape notice, or playing dead, or evolving our appearance (similar colors like the king snake). We may do the same things, literally and/or figuratively.

If we are afraid because something is happening and we don't have enough information to determine what to do, we seek out that information so that we may decide. Covid-19 was and is scary. What do we do? Absent accurate information, we may rely on disinformation. That may not end well. And as we've seen, we may be reluctant to change our minds after we've made a decision, no matter how much new and better information we have. Humans can be stubborn like mules.

## Simplify

We also don't like complex. The acronym KISS (Keep It Simple, Stupid) is popular for a reason. The easier things are, the better able we are to make decisions. Think about it this way: If I ask my husband what he wants for dinner, I don't give him 100 choices, I give him two, maybe three. Why? The more options or the more difficult the decision, the more taxing it may be. I don't say, how about pizza or burgers or tacos or sushi or salads or sandwiches or souvlaki or roast beef. I say, how about pizza or tacos? Speaking of food, how many of you look for recipes that are simple to prepare and require few ingredients? Probably most of you. We have limited time and energy and don't want to expend it making complex decisions. Keep it simple.

If we see something that seems complex that we know little about, we search for the simple answer. If I don't know anything about vaccines, I could seek out information from the CDC or I can go to Robert Kennedy's website which seems to present information in a much simpler way. I don't necessarily care which is more accurate. Which one makes sense?

## Create "Community"

As much as I love my solitude, I also need to belong to a community. All of us do because humans are inherently gregarious creatures. We need to feel that sense of belonging. We want to find others who believe as we do. We seek them out online because social media is the great equalizer. It helps us to find our people and our groups. There is a group for nearly any interest or any belief. And there are many people in those groups. You are not alone. While you may feel alone in your physical community, you may find like-minded others online.

Once we find that group, we may be encouraged to believe everything they believe, since we obviously have so much in common anyway. Groupthink. You may also find yourself wanting to belong more than you want to determine the truth. Our faith, whether it is in a higher power, or faith in our friends, family, and community, is powerful. We want to make sense of the world and ask questions. When we don't have answers—the information void—we seek out those answers in several ways including via a group.

## THE ROLE OF TRAUMA

There is one factor related to disinformation belief I haven't referenced that is often overlooked, and that is trauma. Trauma could be personal trauma, cultural trauma and/or historical trauma. What do I mean?

Suppose as a woman, I was sexually assaulted by my male doctor. That would be traumatizing. I would be reluctant to return to any doctor based on that interaction. Are all doctors going to assault me? Of course not. That doesn't matter. I have personal trauma that is going to be difficult to overcome no matter what facts, science, data, or statistics you share with me. This may also be referred to as availability bias. We look to a recent or vivid event to help us to make decisions. Certainly, sexual assault would qualify as a vivid event.

Suppose I am a Black woman. Not only have I likely had my own personal trauma, but historically and culturally Black people have been abused by the medical system (as well as others). The Tuskegee syphilis experiments scared us and scarred us. They were conducted on unwitting Black men before there was a cure for syphilis. Even when penicillin was found to work wonders, the "participants" weren't given that option. The experiments by James Marion Sims, considered the "father of modern gynecology," were horrific and were conducted on Black slave women, obviously without their consent. If this is how an entire group of people has historically been treated, is it any wonder they don't trust modern medicine?

Guess what it all comes back to?

Trust.

Those social, economic and political structures exploit historical traumas. We still have the building blocks in place to discriminate and discourage participation. Our beliefs drive more than we would likely admit. I spoke with Santi Indra Astuti, lecturer in the faculty of communication science in the Department of Journalism at Bandung Islamic University, Bandung City, Indonesia, and cofounder of Mafindo, a non-profit dedicated to combating hoaxes and disinformation, about disinformation in Indonesia. She is facing many of the same obstacles we face in the United States and for the same reasons. We are not so different globally. She did note that we want to isolate the other, and one way to do that is to share disparaging stereotypes. For example, during Covid-19 one ethnic group in Indonesia was trying to dissuade its members from buying goods from another marginalized group by highlighting how unhygienic the other group was. Santi said it was funny because that other group is generally thought to be quite clean. We will say and do what we need to in order to achieve our end goals. We look to cultural, racial, gender, and political differences to divide us rather than to seek the truth and to understand that we are more alike than not. We lie inside our echo chamber and breath air from our filter bubbles.

## DON'T FEED THE DISINFORMATIONISTS!

Those are just some examples. There are scads more. To help to combat disinformation, it is important to understand which of the above reasons to believe is in play. Then use the same tactics in an ethical and honest way to dissuade.

If we think about our own social framework, what does that look like? We have our traditional social structures like our family, religion, politics, economics, and education. We also have other groups we may identify with like sports and mass media. We look to our peers, family, close friends, school, churches, and other organizations. We also identify based on what we are born with like race/ethnicity, sex, sexuality, and class, but then also identify with what we work toward like occupation, gender, income, and education. These groups coupled with the reasons to belong and believe make for a complicated but interesting infodemic stew.

During the pandemic it was so very easy for us to dismiss people and their beliefs based on political party, for example. Yes, there are data that indicate political party affiliation was a factor in what people believed. But if that was all you paid attention to, you missed trauma and other causes. You fed the infodemic.

It is also easy to dismiss people as stupid. If that's the crux of your argument, you've failed and been stupidly dismissive. Beliefs are much more complex. Fear is complex. Trauma is complex.

Trust is earned.

I've shared data regarding how polarized we are globally. Trust has been eroded. We don't like our neighbors if they are different. Think about what our differences may be. We may differ culturally, racially, religiously, politically, socioeconomically, sexually, to name just a few.

We need to recognize that we all want the same things in the end. We want to feel safe and free from fear. We want to belong. We want to be able to house, clothe, and feed our families and ourselves. We need to understand the "other," but we are being told to fear and distrust the "other."

This is how it spreads. Now let's stop it.

# How Do We Inoculate Ourselves Against Disinformation?

**AS I JUST DISCUSSED**, disinformation is sexy, or can be. How do we dress up the truth so it's just as sexy? It's difficult. I am creative, but even I have a difficult time with this.

I was invited to share information about disinformation in the class of a colleague recently. I mentioned that a common conspiracy theory is the existence of aliens and government cover-up. I also noted that the US government declassifying documents regarding this doesn't help other conspiracy theories because people may say, "See! This conspiracy may be real. Others may also be real!" My colleague then chimed in with, "I've seen a UFO." The entire class stopped listening to me and started peppering him with questions about it. When someone then asked how we should respond to disinformation, I noted how difficult it can be. They proved my point because once we heard someone may have seen a UFO, it was all over for my talk about disinformation. As communicators, we need to be as sexy as UFOs.

How do I share the truth here, being just as "sexy?" What is the truth? Remember the story I told in Chapter 2 about the professor? What if I categorized that as, "Humanities professor uses his sense of humor to get his class to think." That's not nearly as sexy as, "Humanities professor calls students 'disease vectors' and gets fired." Also remember that we don't want to take something out of context, nor do we want a rush to judgment to cloud our thinking. It can be difficult when we know that the salacious is what gets noticed, talked about, and shared. Can we give truth the same treatment to encourage an interest in it?

In this chapter I will discuss how to craft messages to combat disinformation and engage your audience with the truth.

## BEWARE OF FEAR MESSAGING

I've been thinking about fear messaging in relation to disinformation quite a bit lately. Fear messaging is certainly not new. We've seen fear campaigns throughout history. Historic witch hunts come to mind (see more on this in the next chapter).

Fear messaging is any message in any medium (radio, TV, social media, print, etc.) that elicits a fear reaction in the recipient. It's designed to do that. It wants you to be so afraid that you take the proscribed action in the message. For example, "Covid-19 is deadly and if you don't get the vaccine you will die."

That's terrifying. Yes, we all know we will die—that's life. But we would rather it happen later than sooner and perhaps not by a horrific virus. That said, is there truth to the fear message? Yes. It is quite possible that if you contract Covid-19 and you are not vaccinated, you will die. You may not, but the odds are likely against you.

We often see fear messaging in health-related contexts, but health is hardly the only thing to make us fearful. Elections are coming up in the US (and in many other countries) so we see all kinds of fear messaging in political campaigns. "If you don't vote for X candidate, Medicare will no longer exist, and our grandparents will die a slow death in alleys while their kidneys are harvested." That's terrifying! I don't want my grandmother to die alone, and she needs her kidneys for her renal health!

That example seems farfetched, but some of the messaging I see isn't that far off. It is designed to prey on your fears and those crafting the messages do a great deal of research to know exactly which buttons to push. Part of me is appalled by the use of research in such an evil way but another part of me is actually impressed that it is at least being done. That said, not all fear messaging is intended to be evil (or intended to be disinformation). Much of it is actually designed to help.

Do you remember the "This is your brain on drugs" public service announcement by the Ad Council? That's an example of fear messaging and it's an example of fear messaging done very well. It hit the sweet spot in fear messaging—eliciting a medium level of fear (there are also, as you might guess, low and high fear levels). It wasn't too tame by, for example, making people think of breakfast and wanting to add a side of bacon, and it wasn't too harsh causing people to turn away and not get the message at all. It was just right—the Baby Bear of ad campaigns.

In contrast, the SPCA public service announcements narrated by Sarah McLachlan are high fear, at least for me. I see the dog in the cage on the screen, hear the starting refrain for her song "Angel" and I have to change the channel. I cannot watch because I cannot see abused animals. That, to me, is too much. I understand the message and the method behind it, but I just can't.

Fear messaging generally contains information about some harm that may befall the recipient if that person takes no action, and includes a suggested action to take to avoid and/or prevent the harm.

If you don't perceive the risk to be great, you may not take any action. When Covid-19 first arrived on the scene, it was believed that those who were older than sixty-five, or those with co-morbidities or pre-existing conditions were at greater risk and that young, healthy people had nothing to worry about. There was no harm to young people, so no action needed to be taken by them. Let's cast aside transmission for a moment because remember that young people could still carry the virus and kill grandma.

It's also important to know and understand what people are afraid of in order to craft messaging to scare the crap out of them. Many people are afraid of change in one form or another. They are afraid of failure and loss. They are afraid of losing control. They are afraid of the unknown. That's why some of these messages resonate so well. They play on our fears.

Let's return to Covid-19. When more was known about Covid-19 and it became clear that those under sixty-five who are overweight might be at higher risk of contracting Covid-19 and perhaps dying, it scared me! I am over fifty and overweight! I saw that some harm might befall me, so I took the suggested actions. I wore my mask (and still do sometimes) to protect myself and others. I isolated as much as was practical. I jumped into a lifestyle change to lose weight. Then I fell off that wagon and stress ate potato chips and ice cream (not together, that's gross). I think you get the point.

## KNOW YOUR INFLUENCERS

It also matters how we value the opinions of others. We certainly have our own beliefs, but do we also take into account the beliefs of those in our "circles?" Do we care what our parents think or our friends or coworkers or doctors? If so, that may play a role in whether we intend to choose a particular behavior.

The Theory of Reasoned Action, posited by Martin Fishbein and Icek Ajzen in 1975, helps to explain the influencers in our lives. There are four main components: belief, attitude, subjective norms, and intention. Each of us has beliefs about different things. Those beliefs are buffered by our attitudes about those particular beliefs. Subjective norms are the weight we give to outside influences and intention is the result of all three working together.

I will use my weight-loss journey as an example. I believe that if I weigh less, I will have better health. I will have less back and knee pain. I will feel healthier. (Beliefs.) I believe that eating better and exercising will help me achieve this goal. (Attitudes.) I think my family would like it if I felt better about myself. My husband would like me to feel better. Society won't look down on me. (Subjective norms.) I will eat better and work out more because it will make me feel better. I care about what my family thinks but I don't care what society has to say. (Intention.)

So, how do you evaluate fear messages in a similar way? I would argue that you should treat them as you would any other message. Remember in Chapter 4 I noted how to evaluate messages and information? Authority, purpose, publication and format, relevance, date of publication, and documentation—those are your barometers.

We are bombarded with so much information every day it can be difficult to sift through the clutter to find what's real and what's relevant for each of us. It would be worth it, though, to take the steps outlined above and do your own due diligence.

In discussing the theory of reasoned action, we should also reference cognitive dissonance. Cognitive dissonance deals with our own inconsistencies. Let's go back to my weight. I know that if I eat well and exercise, I will lose weight. At the very least I will feel better. Do I eat well and exercise? Not always. What's my weakness? Potato chips and ice cream (again, not together). I can justify the ice cream because women need calcium and you find calcium in ice cream, so eating it is fine. Also, potato chips are just potatoes and potatoes are vegetables so, again, I'm good. I clearly struggle with cognitive dissonance. I behave counter to my own best interests and what I want my behaviors to be. I sometimes call this the "Theory of Justification of Actions." We justify our actions when they run counter to what we know we should do.

## UNPACKING MOTIVATIONS WITH MASLOW

Since we are talking about behaviors, let's talk about what motivates people. Maslow's Hierarchy of Needs Theory details what motivates us. You likely need to start at the bottom of the pyramid. Think about basic needs. We need food, water, clothing, and shelter. We want to feel a sense of belonging. We need to feel protected. What we believe and how we achieve those things may vary, but we all want them. Maslow's pyramid is noted in **Figure 3** (see next page).

Maslow's Hierarchy of Needs details what motivates us in our personal life. Professionally, we may refer to Herzberg's Motivators. What motivates us in the workplace? Herzberg proposed that hygiene factors and motivator factors matter. Hygiene factors include money, benefits, policies, work/life

**FIGURE 3:** Maslow's Hierarchy of Needs

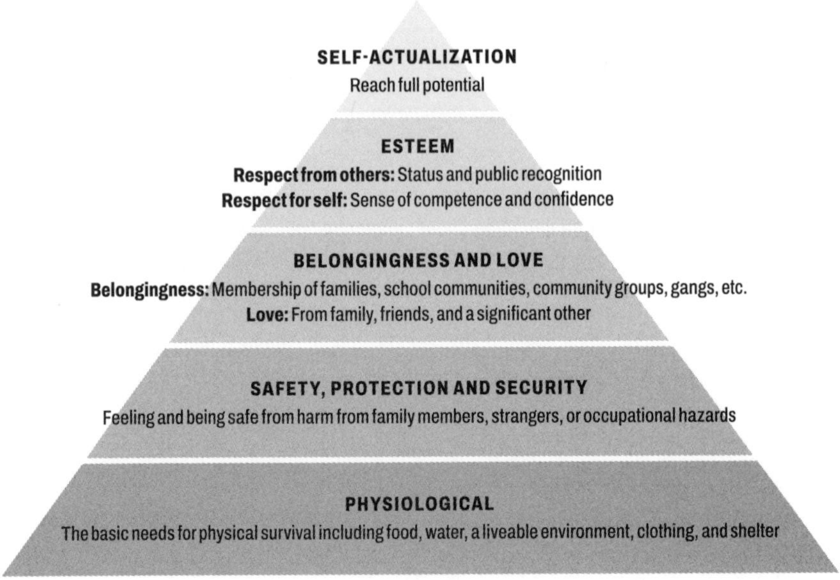

**SELF-ACTUALIZATION**
Reach full potential

**ESTEEM**
**Respect from others:** Status and public recognition
**Respect for self:** Sense of competence and confidence

**BELONGINGNESS AND LOVE**
**Belongingness:** Membership of families, school communities, community groups, gangs, etc.
**Love:** From family, friends, and a significant other

**SAFETY, PROTECTION AND SECURITY**
Feeling and being safe from harm from family members, strangers, or occupational hazards

**PHYSIOLOGICAL**
The basic needs for physical survival including food, water, a liveable environment, clothing, and shelter

balance, and job security. Motivator factors include recognition, challenge, opportunity, and growth. Interestingly, managers will say employees are motivated by money. Sure, that factors into it, but employees are more motivated by what they may get out of work. They want to be respected. They want to feel as though their work matters. They want to feel as though they belong. Think about what motivates and matters to us. If we care about feeling safe and belonging it should come as no surprise that those are things we try to obtain and attain. Fear messaging and us-against-them messaging are powerful and appeal to what we care about.

Once we are motivated, how are we persuaded? Generally, we need to have knowledge. We need to be aware. We need to know there is an issue or problem. Then we need to see messaging that persuades us. That messaging should appeal to what it is that motivates us into paying attention to what we want and need. Then we decide and implement that decision. We then evaluate whether the decision was a good one. We are either satisfied or may go back to the beginning to obtain more knowledge.

It all comes back to motivation, persuasion, and behaviors. Those aren't necessarily easy nuts to crack. Motivation, persuasion, and behaviors affect us in a number of areas in our lives like health, religion, economics, and politics.

If we consider politics, we can look to election disinformation in the US (as well as elsewhere in the world). Disinformation surrounding elections is not new (remember Jefferson and Adams?). What does it look like?

It turns out that democracy in the United States is in peril no matter where you look. According to Republicans, if Democrats are elected, the world will end. According to Democrats, if Republicans win, the world will end. How do you process that?

Let's think about some of the things we've already learned about how that relates to motivation. What is it that people are seeking? People want a sense of community. They want to feel as though they belong somewhere and rallying around a political party and its ideologies is one way to feel a sense of belonging.

People are also fearful, and fear is a powerful motivation. There are any number of things to fear: the future of health care, inflation, the economy, supply chain woes, eroding of civil rights, crime, and safety to name just a few. Add to that the narrative that there is rampant voter fraud, and you have a recipe for chaos and an environment ready for disinformation and conspiracy theories.

## DISINFORMATION AND ELECTIONS

How do you talk to people who espouse disinformation and conspiracy theories, particularly related to voting and elections? Let's unpack a couple of common pieces of disinformation.

I often hear that people may vote more than once because they may get more than one absentee ballot and may also then vote in person. This would be nearly impossible to pull off. To request an absentee ballot, you need to note why you need one. I just did this and was able to vote with an absentee ballot because I was working a poll not in my voting district and was not available during any early voting hours. Often people who request absentee ballots are those who are not in their voting jurisdiction on election day. A great example—those serving in the military. Would you deny any of those serving in our armed services their right to vote? You also have one name on file with your one signature. I suppose you could try to register as someone else, but that would be difficult to do. You may show up at your polling place and vote in person even if you've requested and submitted an absentee ballot but if you do, you will be told that you already voted. You may still be able to vote, but then the system will note that you have voted in person and will discard/destroy/disregard the absentee ballot you sent in. (Note: this may vary with county and state and is US-centric.)

Let's go back to registering as more than one person. Could you do that? I guess you could. I would think that if you are going to go through the trouble to be multiple people that you are going to complete more than one credit card application and go on a shopping spree rather than try to rig an election, but you do you. (Not that I am advocating crime.) Think about the number of people who would need to do this to "steal" an election. That's some pretty good community and relationship building. Also, you need an address. It might be suspect to any Boards of Election if 100 people are living in a small apartment, for example. Or if no abode exists at the address you use. (I tried to find information about using a P.O. box and could not readily find any. Even P.O. boxes have physical addresses tied to them, though.)

So how do you talk to someone who believes this? You could start by asking them why they feel that way. "Why do you think people are able to vote more than once?" Truly listen to what they have to say. I can't stop you from thinking, "Wow, this person is stupid," but please don't say it. Generally speaking, people aren't stupid. They have legitimate reasons for believing as they do and if you approach it from a place of "stupid," you lose an opportunity to learn, empathize, and educate. You may hear a response like, "I know a guy who saw someone vote in the morning and then come back in the afternoon." You could dig to get more details. "Where was this? Are you sure the person voted twice and didn't just show up to say hi to an election worker? Did anyone else notice this?" Those are just a couple of examples. Please don't act all high and mighty and belittle. People can sense that, and they don't like it.

Let's take another example. I have had people come into our polling place asking if our voting machine is hooked to the internet because there are plenty of people who've said that outside entities are hacking our systems and taking votes away and adding votes for different candidates.

Let me explain how voting machines work. In our county we use Dominion Voting Machines (yes, I have read all about the "problem" with Dominion and am pleased with the outcome of the defamation lawsuit). We have paper ballots that voters complete. Those ballots are then scanned into the machines which count the votes and give us a tally at the end of the election. Those paper ballots are then saved to be counted by hand, should that be required. Paper ballots are not altered in any way by the machine or by any election workers (they are marked in ink). Absentee ballots would be the same—marked in ink. Presumably, in states in which voting is done by absentee ballot only, those ballots would be run through a machine and/or hand counted. Even if someone hacked into a machine you wouldn't be able to change votes. And if that did happen, you would have the unaltered paper ballots. (Our machine isn't hooked to the internet in any way. It's plugged into the wall. We don't have internet access where we are.) It would take some skills I am unaware of for the voting machine to change votes and erase ink-marked dots and make new ink marks for other candidates.

If someone shares this piece of disinformation with you, approach them in the same way you would in my first scenario. Try to get at the heart of the problem and provide information that will be helpful for the individual you are speaking with.

One way to do that is to consider how people generally approach new and different information. Or how do people approach a crisis? **Figure 4** highlights the initial reactions people have to a piece of news. Let's suppose a company must recall a product. Initially, you will have about 45 percent of the population who are favorable toward the company and 45 percent who are not favorable. About 8 percent are in the middle and haven't necessarily decided. Then you have the 1 percent on either end that really love you or really hate you. If you are crafting messages, who do you think you should pay attention to?

**FIGURE 4:** Initial Reactions

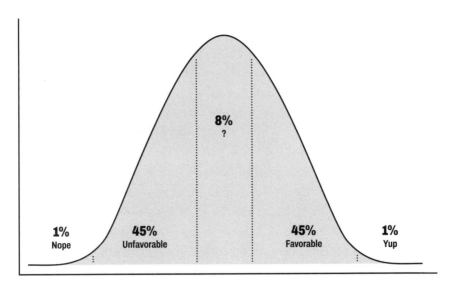

The 45 percent who view you unfavorably and the 8 percent on the fence. You might craft a message for the 45 percent who are favorable but with limited resources, you may not. The 1 percent on either end? Don't bother.

A political example may illustrate this best. Let's suppose the above represents both US political parties (though I would argue the percentage representing the middle or undecides may be higher but work with me for example's sake). Forty-five percent on either side support the Republican or Democrat; 8 percent in the middle are undecided. The 1 percent on either end really like their candidate (and this number is also likely higher than represented here). Are you going to sway those who are staunch Donald Trump supporters to vote for Joe Biden? Not anymore than you are going to sway those who are staunch Joe Biden supporters to vote for Donald Trump. You aren't even going to waste time or money on trying to do so. You are going to target your communication resources to reach those you have a chance of persuading.

What else should you care about when combating disinformation?

- **Know your audience.** Who are you speaking with? What do you know about them? What motivates them? What are they fearful of? What community do they belong to or feel most comfortable in?

- **Know the truth.** Do you have facts, studies, figures, other information? Is that what will appeal to your audience?
- **Do not jump to "stupid."** People aren't generally stupid. There could be any number of reasons for believing what they believe. Try to get to that.

Of course, you may also just walk away from the argument. You are not going to get everyone to believe the truth. Remember that about 1 percent of the population lies on either side (right or left) of conspiracies and ideologies like this and they are not easily persuaded. Save your energy to combat disinformation that is combatable.

## LISTENING AND HEARING

Now I want to unpack listening and hearing. I often speak about both and tell people that to be an effective communicator, you need to both listen and hear. Often my audience will say, "they are the same thing." They are also incorrect. (My audience is not stupid. Remember, we are not stupid.)

Hearing is what we are probably all doing when someone speaks (or when we passively look at nonverbal cues like folded arms, crossed legs, etc.). I hear that noises are coming from your mouth, and I see that your lips are moving, but I am not necessarily "listening." Perhaps I am waiting until your lips and the noises stop so that I may jump in because what I have to say is obviously much more important than your feeble utterances. Perhaps you have alienated me in some way, and I have just tuned you out. Perhaps I am bored. Perhaps…any number of distractions or "noise" is preventing me from truly focusing on your words, expressions, and actions.

Listening, on the other hand, involves action. I need to truly focus and pay attention to what it is you are saying, how you are saying it, why, where, when, all the things. Are you crying as you share your story? Are you laughing? Angry? Frustrated? Do you seem level-headed and calm, but your stance and facial expressions tell me you are anything but?

As communicators we are fond of saying that we "give voice to the voiceless" when referring to the marginalized. I have railed against that phrase, and I am not alone (Anahi Ayala Iacucci,[21] JoAnna Haugen[22] are just two voices speaking out against this phrase). To say that you are giving a voice implies that one didn't have a voice to begin with. In fact, the opposite is true. They have voices; they've just been ignored. They have been neither heard nor listened to.

Imagine that for a second. You have been screaming and no one is listening. Sure, some people may nod politely or even say something like, "thoughts and prayers," or "I understand" when in fact they have no understanding whatsoever. Imagine not being understood and not understanding how to rephrase or restate in a way that aids understanding. Imagine just being ignored and/or forgotten.

Are you going to trust someone who has repeatedly ignored you but who suddenly seems to care? Of course you aren't. You are likely immune to any correspondence from those people.

Have you had interactions in the past in which you may have pooh-poohed, laughed at, belittled, or ignored someone? Or have they done this to you? Think about how you might interact with them now.

## PERCEPTIONS

What role do people's perceptions play in decision-making? If people perceive something to be true, it's true for them. Doesn't matter that it may not be true. A common visual example of perceptions I like to use may been seen in **Figure 5**.

What do you see when you look at this image? You should see two things: two faces (in the white space) and a vase (in the black space). If you don't see both of those, look again. If my job is to get you to see the entire picture and all you see are two faces, we have a problem. I have to figure out how to communicate that there is also a vase.

I've worked with people in the past who've said they are sick of hearing about perceptions and don't care what people perceive. That's sad and dangerous. It doesn't matter what you want and care about. If you need to get people to see the entire picture, you better figure out how to do that.

**FIGURE 5:** Perception

You must both listen and hear.

How do you do that? Focus on what that person is saying, try to understand why they are saying it or where they are getting the information, focus on your relationship with this person, and focus on the truth. Again, it's not the time for you to show off all the fancy polysyllabic (tee hee) words you know. Nor is it the time for you to recite your CV/resume.

Hear them.

Listen.

Understand.

That does not mean you agree, nor does it mean that you condone behaviors. It means you are making an effort to understand the rationale behind the thinking. Also, recognize your own biases and shortcomings. Could you be wrong in some way?

Think, too, about whether the behavior, phrases, or thinking are dangerous or just shortsighted. If it's dangerous you might need to act. If it's just shortsighted, perhaps let it go. If you have a friend who believes in aliens, that's probably not the worst thing, unless your friend is risking his life sitting in the backyard in the cold waiting to be abducted or some similar scenario. (And aliens may exist.) If, however, your friend is preventing his relatives from getting a lifesaving vaccine that's another story that may require big figurative guns. That may require that you listen to his concerns about why he feels this is the right treatment option. It will certainly require that you know the person well enough to know what will motivate or persuade him. It absolutely requires empathy, listening, and trust.

## THE ROLE OF MEDIA

We've talked about the media quite a bit throughout, but we haven't really discussed the role of the media. The rhetoric has been "fake news" and "mainstream media." Let's look at who really works in media and how they affect our perception of reality.

### Journalists

I have shared that I have worked with journalists for years. I am the former dean of a school of communication which includes journalism education. We have been training journalists for over seventy years. Contrary to what people may be led to believe, journalists hold themselves to a series of ethical guidelines. As with any profession, are there those who don't? Yes, but they are few and far between. The problem with that is their voices tend to get elevated every time there is an issue or problem, so that it is assumed to be the norm.

For example, Jayson Blair was a young *New York Times* journalist who was fired in 2003 because he was found to be plagiarizing or inventing content. The *Times*' tagline is "All the News That's Fit to Print." It prides itself on quality, ethical journalism. This was an embarrassment. This was also one person out of hundreds working at the paper at the time. Would we want one person to represent us? Not likely.

Another prominent story is the 2014 *Rolling Stone* story about the University of Virginia men who allegedly raped a woman. The "reporter" made it up. We could argue that the news outlets need to do a better job of fact-checking, but here is another example of a piece with profound implications for the organization.

Trust was eroded in both cases. Some still talk about both cases even though they happened years ago and have been remedied and rectified. They stick with us just as past science and medicine information sticks with us. Put cocaine back in Coca-Cola!

Journalists adhere to a code of ethics to tell the truth. Journalists help us to understand what is going on in the world and in our own backyards. They are trained in excellent communication skills but are also trained in ethics. Getting it right trumps getting it first.

Journalists hold truth to power. Think of the countries in which there is no free press. Generally, you are talking about dictatorships. People are not free. Those who don't like journalists are often those with something to hide or who have faced the firing squad of a journalist's pen. Journalists hold people, especially our elected officials, accountable. They set aside their biases to report the truth. They inform people about the issues. They educate the masses so that we may make informed choices. They play an integral role in communicating what we need to know about a number of topics. Many become subject-matter experts. A colleague of mine who worked in public relations used to say, "if you don't want bad publicity, don't do stupid shit." That seems to be a reasonable prescription.

## PR and Communication

In addition to the work of journalists, I look to those who work in public relations or other communication-related fields. So much of our understanding of the infodemic comes down to communication. Do we have the information we need? Can we fill the voids?

When the Covid-19 pandemic brought the infodemic to the fore, I couldn't help but think about how I would respond from a crisis communication perspective. I consider the infodemic to be a crisis. What steps do we take in a crisis to inform and calm?

There are generally four stages in a crisis: warning stage, point of no return, cleanup phase, and things return to normal (with a caveat). There is always a warning, though you often don't see it until after—hindsight being 20/20. Once you get to the point of no return you have to ride the crisis roller coaster to its end. This is where you really do need to act. Once the crisis has ridden through, you clean up the mess left behind.

Then you return to normal. However, that normal is rarely what it was before the crisis, rather it is a new normal. With any luck (and skill), you learned something from the crisis that you don't repeat in the future. I keep wondering what we've learned from the pandemic that we might not repeat the next time. And there will be a next time. If we think the Covid-19 pandemic is the last pandemic, we are kidding ourselves. I am not saying that to scare and sow fear. I am saying that because…science.

Crisis may take many forms. You may have acts of God, like storms and forest fires. You may have mechanical problems like the lead pipes in Flint, Michigan. You may have human error or improper management decisions like not sounding the alarm early enough to save people's lives in the case of Covid-19 or impending disasters. Perhaps there are rumors and scandals. There could also be violence or terrorism.

When a crisis happens, we may refer to **Figure 5** and note that you will always have those who view your crisis favorably or unfavorably; those who lean one way or another; and those on the fence. As with other communication, you are going to try to reach those who view you unfavorably and who are on the fence.

Crisis communicators also have many tactics at their disposal to help allay fears and avert or quell the crisis. Some of these include:

- **Pre-emptive action (prebuttal).** If you can get in front of the news and own it, you are much better off. This requires that you have social listening tools in place to be able to predict or at least know that the warning stage is near. Dr. Gounder's response to her husband's death with an editorial is an example of a prebuttal.
- **Offensive response (attack, embarrassment, shock, threat).** I don't generally recommend this strategy because it forces you to go on the attack. You may employ it if you do feel embarrassed or shocked by whatever incident. If you feel threatened, well, figure it out. Don't put the onus to solve that problem on others. You may see an organization express shock when it finds out one of its own has behaved badly. Catholic Church?
- **Defensive response (denial, excuse, justification).** Deny if you truly did nothing wrong. I always advocate for the truth in all

dealings. Making excuses is fine, but that may make you look like you aren't solving a problem and are pointing a finger. Own your mess. You may justify if it helps solve the problem. Don't justify so you look less bad. You may see an organization express shock when it finds out one of its own has behaved badly. Boy Scouts of America ring a bell?

- **Diversionary response (concession, ingratiation, disassociation, relabeling).** Conceding is nice. Ingratiating is pandering. Disassociation and relabeling makes you look guilty or clueless. If two groups are working together and one does something illegal, the other group may disassociate with the organization and be public about it, so they are not "guilty by association."
- **Vocal commiseration (concern, condolences, regret, apology).** Certainly express concern, offer condolences, and express regret if that's how you feel. Be careful with apologies because your legal team may caution against it. Apologies may be considered admissions of guilt.
- **Rectifying behavior (investigation, corrective action, restitution, repentance).** If you are fixing things, note that. If something goes wrong in an organization, the CEO or other leader may come forward to detail that an investigation is ongoing and that corrective action will be taken.
- **Deliberate inaction (strategic silence, strategic ambiguity).** If you say "no comment," I assume you are guilty. If you have developed relationships with your audience and have established a level of trust, "no comment" gets you nowhere. You can explain that you may not be able to comment because you need more information or you have to wait until names have been released, etc. Make sure you offer an explanation—and a timeframe when you anticipate being able to speak. You may see this written up in a news article as, "the person didn't respond to repeated requests for comment," or something to that effect.

With any crisis, there is opportunity. Sometimes heroes are born (thank you, Dr. Fauci). Change may be accelerated. Latent problems are fixed. People can change. New strategies evolve. Early warning systems develop. New competitive edges appear. During the pandemic I watched very closely at how businesses handled the economic downturn and the shutdowns. Those who were able to adapt and pivot did very well. For example, those restaurants who were able to remain open and offer their food to go rather than eat in, fared pretty well. Businesses who were able to transition to online ordering or to pick-up services also did pretty well. One of our local restaurants told us that business was better than ever during the pandemic because they were able to make the shift and quickly. They are still open.

Buffalo, New York, suffered a catastrophic blizzard at Christmastime in 2022. Warnings were issued up to a week ahead of the storm, yet many people died. A post-blizzard task force revealed cracks in the warning system that have been remedied (we hope) for the next blizzard. Early warning systems were developed. It might be argued that latent problems in the system were also fixed.

Change was accelerated in national elections during the pandemic. Many states that didn't have widespread absentee balloting or early voting instituted those measure. Many remain in place.

You may be wondering why on Earth I decided to give you a lesson in journalism and crisis communication. I wanted to strut my stuff and preen my peacock feathers. That's not true. I find both incredibly important in the context of the infodemic. It is imperative that people understand the role of journalists because so much necessary information is communicated via news outlets, yet many people don't understand what goes into being a journalist. I've just given you the tip of the iceberg here.

So how do we as consumers of information know whom to trust in "the media?" Start with good social listening practices. What is that exactly? Social listening requires that you pay attention to what is being said vocally, in writing, on social media, in broadcast media, in your church, on the street. It involves listening and hearing everything. It is easy for people to look at comments and posts on social media, but much of our communication also takes place across the backyard fence. No one is listening to it except those involved. We are interested in all the conversations especially those we can't see, hear, and access easily. They are the most interesting and the ones that will yield the most information about what people really think, what scares them, and what emotions are driving their decisions.

We do have some ways of working around this. One is to rely on the opinion leaders. These may be teachers at school, leaders in church, coaches, bartenders, stylists, and others. We also have Google. Studies indicate that Google may be able to predict disease outbreaks just based on what searches are trending. For example, many of us turn to "Dr. Google" when we feel ill. We will Google our symptoms to see what we may have before we make an appointment with our physician. Often these search trends may indicate what disease may be prevalent and where. One may consider this an invasion of privacy, but I'd like to stress that it isn't as though Google knows that Pauline Hoffmann searched her symptoms and found out that she has Covid-19 and then sent her street address to people. Google looks at information in the aggregate and may note how many people in the Southern Tier of New York State Googled similar symptoms. Then we can just lob off that section of the state and cede it to Pennsylvania. (I'm joking.)

Our words and deeds do matter. We need to be authentic, transparent, and truthful at all times. Trust is earned and once lost not easily remedied.

# Stirring Up Disinformation With Witch Hunts

**I AM A PRACTICING WITCH.**

When you read that sentence I am sure a number of visions were conjured in your head. Black robe/cloak. Pointed black hat. Long nose. Green face. Wrinkled fingers. Warts. Cackle for a laugh. Black cat for a pet. Cauldron in the backyard. Children locked in a cage. Eye of newt in my pantry. In fact, I once gave a lecture to first-year undergraduate students about Wicca (my specific practice) and afterward read feedback regarding the talk. One student actually wrote that he normally sat in the front row during class but moved to the back when he heard I was coming because he didn't know what I would do.

I am not quite clear what he thought I might do. Turn him into a frog? Steal his lunch money?

The stereotypes are there and I am aware of them.

In this chapter, in addition to exploring the confluence of science and spirituality, I will touch on the history behind witch hunts, what that means and how the phrase has been absconded in modern parlance. I will also note why witch hunts are important in the context of disinformation.

## LET'S GET WITCHY

Let's go back to explain a bit about what being a witch means.

I don't have a green face nor do I have a long nose. I'm getting older, so I do have wrinkles but not the kind you imagine. I do cackle and sometimes pee a little when I laugh. I don't care for cats. My preferred pets are dogs. I don't like children but wouldn't dream of putting them in a cage even if they pissed me off. I don't have eye of newt in the pantry.

I generally describe Wicca as a religion connected with the natural world. I also note that our credo is "Do what you will but harm none." That sounds a bit like the Golden Rule, and that would be correct. We also believe in the power of three—what we put into the world comes back to us threefold. For example, if I were to abuse my status as a professor, that abuse would come back to me threefold. I don't do that because it is wrong and also, I have no interest in seeing what that may look like.

It also works the other way. If I practice good deeds, that energy will come back to me threefold. Good conquers evil.

There are many different practices a witch may undertake. I noted that I am Wiccan. You may consider yourself Pagan. You may say that you are a green witch or a kitchen witch. You may worship different gods and goddesses from different faith traditions like Norse, Druid, or Egyptian deities. There are many, many ways you may practice and not all are the same. There is no one correct way to practice.

I do cast spells. Before people get all, "I'm gonna be a toad!" I generally say a spell is not too different from a prayer. If you pray, you are casting a spell even though you may not think of it that way. I only cast spells that may impact me or others—with their permission. I don't practice so-called black magic (power of three, remember), nor do I cast love spells or other spells that may alter someone's free will.

One of the reasons the craft, as witchcraft may be called, was so appealing to me is that is allowed me to be who I am and to practice as I like without a proscribed or prescribed methodology. That's funny coming from a scientist who values proscribed and prescribed methodologies. Succinctly put, I am a witch because I value the feminine and masculine energy of the craft as well as the reliance on and reverence for nature in all its glory.

Now that you've had a crash course (and it was a crash course) in Wicca, let's take a look at some original witch hunts.

## HISTORIC WITCH HUNTS

In the United States, the most famous witch hunts took place in Salem, Massachusetts, beginning in 1692. A so-called "witch" was believed to be someone who worshipped and/or followed Satan. (Most modern witches I know do not believe in Satan. We believe in evil but do not personify it.) Witches were primarily women. There were some men who were accused and executed but by and large, the accused were women.

Hindsight being what it is, women were rooted out because they had some power. That power could take a number of forms. Women were often the healers within a group. To be fair, that hasn't changed much. When a child gets hurt, for example, rarely do you hear them yell, "Dad!" Before modern medicine, women often relied on herbal remedies. There is certainly a modern movement to return to those roots, pun intended, but I'm not here to discuss specific herbal remedies. Those remedies were gotten from plants in the forest or in fields. Some remedies seemed miraculous, hence the idea that these women were practicing some form of magic or witchcraft. The thinking behind this was if those in power (men) couldn't figure it out, clearly there was a supernatural element at play, and these women must have made a deal with the devil.

Remember earlier in the book when I discussed the different types of power? I also noted in the history of communication that with each new communication tool, some power is taken from the elite and spread to the masses. We can't have that!

Notorious witch hunts occurred throughout Europe and seemed to pop up every couple of centuries or so. Women, primarily, were persecuted in

Spain, Germany, France, England, Scotland, and Ireland, to name a few. Given that we see present-day witch hunts in other parts of the world, it would be naïve to think that witch hunts haven't occurred throughout history across the globe and not just in Western culture.

The number of people persecuted as witches is unknown. Some cite the figure as low as 10,000 while others estimate it may be in the millions. Often witch hysteria was a result of some sort of religious, political, or cultural fervor. It may also have been triggered by hatred or fear of the "other." The witch hunt in Salem, for example, started with an accusation by young girls who had fits that today may be explained by science (there are a couple of competing theories including ingestion of a fungus or encephalitis). At the time, these fits indicated possession. Someone must have been to blame. Enter scapegoats and accusations against anyone you didn't particularly like or understand.

Sadly, there are some places in the world in which witch hunts still take place by the historic definition. Women, primarily, are still targets. They are accused of witchcraft and are persecuted and/or executed. Every so many years I hear about a child accused of being a witch or of being possessed by the devil who is tortured and eventually killed. In 2020, a 90-year-old woman in Ghana was beaten to death after being accused of being a witch. Sometimes it is in the name of religion; sometimes in the name of culture. Either way, it is still happening. In fact, August 10 has been declared the World Day Against Witch Hunts by the global Pontifical Mission Societies. August 10 is also the day after my birthday. Coincidence?

How did those in power identify witches? There were a number of "tests." I do not know how those in power decided which "tests" would determine if you were a witch or not. One test was whether a woman had the "mark of the devil" on her. These varied from an extra nipple (some people have more than two) which some believed the Devil would use to suckle, to a birthmark. Women were often forced to strip or were forcibly stripped in public to show these alleged "devil marks."

Another test involved tying weights around a woman and tossing her into a nearby body of water. If she sank, she was innocent; if she floated she was a witch.

I'll let you read that sentence again and think about it.

Can you guess what happened? Women died. None of them floated. So, they were innocent but also dead. Ah well. Guess we screwed that one up!

Additionally, if a woman could recite the Lord's Prayer without error or omission, she was deemed innocent. If she was pricked or scratched and didn't bleed or feel pain, she was a witch.

Often, even those women who "passed" these barbaric and ridiculous witch tests weren't exonerated. There was always another level to get past, another goal post moved.

This led to witch hysteria. If all that was needed to be accused of witchcraft was a neighbor saying they saw you with the devil sucking your third nipple, then you were arrested and tried as a witch. Neighbors would accuse each other to prevent being accused themselves or simply because they didn't like you. If you were a bit different, you were a witch because we don't like the "other."

Context is also important. We are looking at what happened historically. Think about what we knew about science and medicine in the fifteenth through eighteenth centuries. Not enough. If we thought that some of the tests were scientific or medically founded, we've come a long way, baby.

If you are operating from a state of fear, it would make sense that you are rushing to judgment. You need to weed out this perceived problem. If you trust Neighbor X and she said that Neighbor Y is a witch, then it must be true. Let's load her pockets up with rocks, toss her in the lake and see what happens. There was so much that was unknown. If women were able to cure ailments that learned men could not, obviously they were witches. Worse, if they could not cure an ailment and the person died, they could be accused of harboring ill intent and may be accused of being a witch anyway. If women were seen with a "creature" suckling at their nipple, obviously it's the devil—if seen from a distance. Never mind that perhaps she's feeding her baby. If a woman didn't quite fit in because she was a bit different or shy, she was a witch.

## THE MODERN 'WITCH HUNT'

We often hear the phrase "witch hunt" used in the media, often when a public figure feels accused of some wrongdoing they did not commit—or claims to have not committed. They feel they are serving as a scapegoat of sorts. It is intended to discredit the accuser by suggesting that the attack or investigation is politically, personally, commercially, or otherwise motivated.

We have heard the phrase bandied about in recent years. Woody Allen described the public shaming and subsequent persecution of Harvey Weinstein as a "witch hunt." Donald Trump has continued to say he is a victim of multiple "witch hunts," particularly with his criminal and civil indictments.

The phrase may also be used when mass hysteria surrounds a particular topic. When US politicians referred to Covid-19 as the "China Virus," it fomented hatred around Asian Americans—a witch hunt. After September 11, 2001, there was much hatred aimed at Muslims within the US— another witch hunt. Immigrants to the US who are not white are often singled out for one reason or another, particularly when the narrative is that they are rapists, drug dealers and/or terrorists—another witch hunt. The war in Gaza has highlighted a case of witch hunt hysteria. Both Jews and Palestinians are accused in one way or another—a modern witch hunt.

What happens in a case of hysteria? You see people not involved in the conflict at all being ridiculed, bullied, tormented, harassed, harmed, and even killed. In each example referenced above, people from one ethnic and/or religious group were targeted and ridiculed, bullied, tormented, harassed, harmed, and killed. And it continues.

## WITCH HUNTS AS DISINFORMATION

I would like to unpack this a bit further. Think about what I've written in this chapter. Specifically:

- A particular group (in this case, women) were primarily accused.
- Herbal remedies were used and questioned if too miraculous.
- "Tests" to determine if someone was a witch were developed and used (and were nonsensical).
- Specific groups of people were targeted in the face of some real or perceived harm to a large group.
- In all cases, hysteria ensued.
- In all cases, reason was abandoned.

Does the above list look familiar? A group of people is targeted. Science is questioned (or at least the science of the time). Accusations and logical fallacies are shared to discredit and shift the narrative. People are fearful and are looking for answers and community. In doing so, they may abandon reason.

Witch hunts are a historic and current disinformation campaign.

Let's be more specific and look closely at a classic example, one that we've talked about **a lot** in this book, Covid-19.

## Covid-19 as the "China Virus"

Covid was detected in China in late 2019. By early 2020, as we all remember, the world closed up shop. It was also at that time that many including politicians and some media were referring to the virus not as Covid but as the Wuhan, China, or Chinese virus. It made some sense since we were comparing it, incorrectly, to the Spanish flu of 1919, which got its name because it was believed to have originated in Spain. That was since disproved, but the name stuck (remember my discussion of nomenclature in Chapter 2). A late 2020 study by Darling-Hammond, et al. examined the marked increase in the use of stigmatizing language on Twitter (now X) and in conservative media outlets. They noted that the increase in stigmatizing language correlated with an increase in anti-Asian American sentiment including a distrust of Asian Americans that may lead to increased anxiety and mental health issues among this marginalized group. We also saw hate crimes committed against Asian Americans. To be fair, anti-Asian hate has never gone away, but it did increase with the increased use of improper language.

What was happening? I've noted that when we first heard about Covid there was so much that was not known, but we did see that people were dying. There was an incredible amount of fear. When we are fearful, we look for an easy and easily explained reason. If this virus started in China, then all Asians were to blame (never mind for a moment that while the population of China is large, not all Asians are Chinese). We needed to exert our power over this group of people. We do not like the "other."

A fear of the "other" is at the heart of the modern-day witch hunt. For those who claim "witch hunt!" when they are actually being held accountable (usually people in positions of power), the "other" is the public at large—particularly members of the public who believe they should answer for their indiscretions and/or crimes. For witch hunts that target specific groups of people in the face of some real or perceived harm to a large group, the targeted group is the "other." And stoking fear about them drives the hysteria that can be dangerous, even deadly, filling our collective pockets with rocks as we sink into the depths of disinformation.

# Elvis Is Alive And Working At A 7-Eleven In Sheboygan

## An Introduction To Conspiracy Theories

**DO YOU THINK** you are immune to disinformation and conspiracy theories? Think again. We may all be susceptible. Certainly, we all think we are much smarter than to be taken in by false information, but be honest with yourself: Have you ever believed something to later find out it was completely untrue? Or the reverse? Have you ever believed so strongly that something was crap, but you later found it to be true? If you approach a situation with the idea that you may be fooled, you may be better able to handle the information than not.

In this chapter I will talk about conspiracy theories, how to identify them and how to talk to others about them. I will also stress that many conspiracy theories are harmless and perhaps funny; others are not.

## BREAKING DOWN CONSPIRACY THEORIES

What is a conspiracy theory? According to Merriam-Webster, it is "a theory asserting that a secret of great importance is being kept from the public." It is something that is secret…and we—the believers—are savvy enough to have uncovered the secret! Bwahhhaaaa! I would argue that in many cases, disinformation may be a conspiracy theory. The reasons people believe in conspiracies may be the same reasons they fall for disinformation campaigns.

I've been speaking to undergraduate students lately about disinformation—what it is, how to recognize it and how to dispel it. As part of that conversation, I reference conspiracy theories. Check out some common conspiracy theories in **Figure 6**. The small circle represents real-life events that **did** happen. As the circles grow, so does the fantastical nature of each type of conspiracy theory, ranging from silly theories to those that put others in danger. Check out Abbie Richards' excellent conspiracy chart for a wealth of examples.[23]

One conspiracy theory I often refer to is Pizzagate. Let me refresh your memories: Alex Jones, et al, "reported" that Hillary Clinton was involved in a pedophilia/porn ring that was housed in the basement of a pizza parlor in DC. A "concerned citizen" decided to take matters into his own hands and showed up at said pizza parlor with weapons to save the children. Apparently, "the media won't report" this pedophilia ring.

Yes, we want children to be safe and we want to protect them. Was this true? Not even a little bit. It scared the pepperoni out of the people working that day, I imagine. Poor pizza dude was probably thinking, "Okay, fine! I'll take the onions off—back off!" Disinformation and conspiracy in action here, working hand in hand.

Cut to many of the mass shootings and other acts of violence in the United States and elsewhere around the world. Often you hear or see that hateful rhetoric spawned the violence.

Disinformation goes beyond just laughing at your drunk uncle who spews untruths. Looking at Richards' conspiracy chart, it is easy to laugh at other conspiracies, but take a look at the way that chart is organized—from speculation to the point of no return. Believing some of these lies can be dangerous as in the Pizzagate conspiracy.

**FIGURE 6:** Common Conspiracy Theories

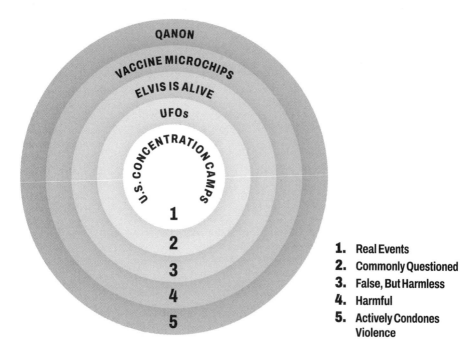

1. **Real Events**
2. **Commonly Questioned**
3. **False, But Harmless**
4. **Harmful**
5. **Actively Condones Violence**

What about aliens? Stop for a second. Reports of unidentified aerial phenomena (UAP—they aren't UFOs anymore) and aliens have been reported for centuries. Also, the universe is vast. It is quite arrogant of us to think we are the only life forms. Also, if the US is declassifying documents related to sightings, there must be something to that, right?

Have I lost all credibility discussing aliens? Do I believe? I don't *not* believe, but I need more evidence than declassified documents. I need to see—though I don't need to be abducted.

## WHY DO SO MANY PEOPLE BELIEVE IN CONSPIRACY THEORIES?

Conspiracy theories are difficult to combat because they often started with a kernel of truth, no matter how small that kernel was. And sometimes, as in the case of aliens, they may prove to be completely true.

A wonderful *New York Times* editorial, by Paul Krugman, titled "Conspiracy Theorizing Goes Off the Rails",[24] noted that conspiracy theories generally take one of two forms: "those that involve a small, powerful cabal, and those that require that thousands of people collude to hide the truth."

I want to unpack that. He used QAnon (a group that believes a secret, small group of pedophiles controls the US government) as the example of a powerful cabal, and climate change (it's a hoax cooked up by thousands of scientists worldwide, some believe) as collusion. There are many, many others. Covid-19 would be an example. The 2020 election would be another. I could go on for days…

I won't.

But why do we believe? There are several reasons, and they mirror the same reasons people believe disinformation—or believe anything.

## Fear

First, conspiracy theories may play to our fears. They target and prey on what we are afraid of. Take the disinformation surrounding vaccines. What are we afraid of? We are afraid of getting the initial disease, yes. But we are also afraid of the unknown. If we don't know how vaccines work, we might fear the rhetoric that vaccines will harm, maim, or kill. We may have an underlying distrust that is just fed by the additional information telling us that we are correct.

## Bias

This leads me to confirmation bias (which you first read about in Chapter 5). We seek out information that reinforces our already held beliefs. If I believe the medical profession seeks to harm me (or ignore me or discredit me) because I am a woman, I may be hesitant to believe them when they tell me vaccines are okay. I may seek out information that supports a medical cabal against women.

## Emotion

We may also be so taken with emotions that we ignore facts and logic (post-truth). Or we may not know how to read and understand the information that's out there. There is much that is shared. It can be incredibly difficult to cull through all the information we are bombarded with daily! This happened with vaccines and vaccine information.

## Partisanship

Partisanship plays a role in disinformation and conspiracy theories. If we believe the rhetoric from our preferred political party, we may not dig deeper and look at the facts. We may be driven by partisan fear and emotion. If we are incredibly upset that our preferred candidate did not win, we may believe disinformation and conspiracies surrounding the loss. No evidence exists of widespread election fraud, yet a number of people believe it to be.

## Complexity

Many disinformation campaigns revolve around incredibly complex issues. We cannot possibly know everything. We can only be an expert in a niche area. What about those areas we are unfamiliar with? Do we have the tools to determine what is real and what is not? I love science, data, and health care. Not everyone does. I hear from people that they loathe those topics. Part of the reason is because they don't understand or they don't think they understand. I even hear people say that they can't comprehend those topics. (Bah! science, data, and health care are for everyone, and it is my life's mission to make you love it!) Conspiracies often arise to simplify complex issues. If someone speaks our "language," we are apt to believe them, particularly about subjects with which we have little or no familiarity.

## ECHO CHAMBERS

There is an echo chamber in our communication universe. We are able to self-select what we hear, read, and see. We are also able to self-select with whom we hang out and listen. That may be to our detriment—but it is certainly understandable. It is much easier to connect with people who are like us than not. It does behoove us to listen to, read, and see others. It is through understanding that we break barriers.

With that echo chamber and with social media algorithms, we are able to live in our own little bubbles. I love that social media has opened the world up to us, but I have to admit that I find myself looking for others who share my values and beliefs.

If you found yourself nodding or saying, "amen" to any of the above does it mean you will fall victim to disinformation and/or conspiracy theories? Maybe, maybe not. Arming yourself with information will help you recognize why you may be believing or willing to believe in certain things. Remember authority, purpose, publication and format, relevance, date of publication, and documentation. Do your due diligence. Care before you share. Check yourself to see if you are resorting to emotion over facts, biases over truth, fear over reason.

All that said, not all conspiracies are dangerous. I love the interactive conspiracy theory in Figure 6 that gives you more information on common conspiracy theories, but also ranks them by possible truth and least dangerous to most dangerous. Also remember that some former conspiracies were determined to be true. It's almost like science fiction eventually becoming nonfiction.

## YOU CAN'T CHANGE EVERYONE'S MIND

Remember, you will not get to everyone. You will not convince everyone of what is right. There are so many, many reasons for that. One of them is that the narrative does sometimes change. Remember the Scientific Method? Science is an evolution. What we know today may not be true tomorrow. Are there universal truths? Yes. We call them laws. Gravity and relativity are two examples. You can believe a law to be untrue (if conspiracy theorists have taught us anything it's that you can believe whatever the hell you want). Doesn't change the law. If you don't believe in gravity, you won't float away. Gravity doesn't care if you believe in it. There are also theories that are damn near laws but need just a bit more. Evolution is one of them. Some argue evolution is bunk. Okay. I may not do much to change your mind. We still have people believing the Earth to be flat. Those same people probably believe the moon landing was faked and those photos showing a round Earth. Fake.

The reality is that people once did think the Earth was flat. Absent information to prove otherwise, they went with what they had. That's science. Absent information to inform us differently, we use what we have to draw conclusions. Sometimes we have to modify those conclusions. That said, once we have abundant information, it becomes more difficult to dispute. I would argue that is the case with evolution. We have much evidence to note that the world was not created in a week but was created over millennia. We also have much evidence to note that climate change is more than real, and humans are driving it.

Let me jump to Covid-19 for a moment. We have much evidence to note that vaccines are effective. We also have much evidence to note how viruses spread and are contracted. However, sometimes we don't have all the information we need right away. Sometimes things take time, and we are an impatient lot! We are so used to having answers at our fingertips (thank you inter webs) that we don't want to wait to get the best results. Then we judge you harshly for "flip-flopping."

I also wonder if sometimes people just don't want to be wrong. I don't like being wrong. It sucks. Luckily it doesn't happen often. Just ask my husband. That's why it is so important to approach the subject gingerly. Telling someone they are stupid never works. Having that tone—and you know that tone—that implies they are stupid also doesn't work. Just ask my husband. What happens in that case? No amount of "evidence" you provide is going to change that person's mind. To be fair, there is often more to it than just not wanting to be wrong. That's the trouble with conspiracies. Let's break one down so I can explain it in more detail.

"Covid-19 was created by the Democrats to shut the world down and help its election outcomes." (I have heard this among other things.) This conspiracy might actually be both types of conspiracy mentioned earlier—a cabal (Democrats) and thousands working together (also Democrats). Politics aside, do you believe either of our political parties is organized enough to do this? Think about the problems we have in the US. If any party was capable of this type of subterfuge, think of what could be accomplished if they used their powers for good, not evil. I could say that to someone and it won't be believed. There will be another layer. They might say, "Well, this is something that is very important to them, so they figured out how to do it." Um, I guess. I still don't have that kind of faith, nor do we have any kind of evidence (belief and science working together there).

People have trouble distinguishing between facts and opinions. Late New York Senator Daniel Patrick Moynihan famously said, "You're entitled to your opinions, but not your own facts." Facts are not refutable. Opinions are your own take. People may certainly take facts and twist them. We see that often. But facts are facts. And there are no "alternative facts." Those are opinions or lies.

Where do we get evidence? I guess that depends on who you trust. We already know who and what we do and do not trust. Evidence suggests that trust in media is decreasing. I have to believe that the fiasco at Fox News isn't helping. Think about that. We now have evidence that folks there haven't been and still aren't adhering to the Society for Professional Journalists' Code of Ethics. Where are people supposed to turn to get accurate information? That's one news outlet but if Fox News is doing that why wouldn't we believe it's happening at other news outlets?

Distilling information for the average audience is also important. I can spew all kinds of numbers and statistics but most people won't have any idea what I'm talking about. To be clear, that doesn't make anyone stupid. We all have our aptitude. I'm not doing quantum physics and would not understand a physicist spewing quantum at me. (I know quantum isn't spewed, but it makes my point. At least I don't think it is. Also making my point.) It takes skill from both sides to breach the barrier. I have to understand that not everyone knows what I know and figure out a way to communicate better. I would also have to understand that I need to know some things in order to comprehend some headier topics. While the latter is important, I put the onus on the expert to share information accurately and effectively. That's not a skill everyone has.

Therein lies the need for a communication liaison, of sorts. Someone who can help digest topics for everyone.

## WHEN CONSPIRACY THEORIES TURN DANGEROUS

It should be stressed that conspiracy theories may harm those who are unwittingly embroiled in them. There is a fantastic example that spawned a podcast (*Tiffany Dover is Dead*) that illustrates this point. Tiffany Dover is one of the first nurses to receive the Covid-19 vaccine. She also had a syncopal episode after getting the shot. What that means is she often has an overactive vagal response to pain. If she gets a shot or experiences other pain, she essentially gets light-headed and faints. That's what happened. You can imagine what conspiracy theorists and anti-vaxxers thought: She actually died and was replaced by a lookalike was the most common assessment. When she tried to dispel this rumor, the theories just escalated. I think some even said it couldn't be her because in some post-vaccine photos, her hair was darker, and she was heavier. Well, pizza, wings, and a good hair stylist could have easily accounted for those changes!

The naysayers forced her to get off social media and isolate. She was hounded by people, and many were vicious. All because she fainted when she got the vaccine. My first thought was: *Hey, hospital, if you knew this might occur, why didn't you pick a different nurse?* Warning stage would be knowing your nurse has this condition. To be fair, though, I don't know that anyone would predict this level of conspiracy. I would have thought some would say the vaccine caused her condition—and some probably did—even though she's lived with it her whole life.

Another example of conspiracies gone off the rails to disgrace involves Amanda Makulec[25] who lost her baby during the pandemic. She expressed her pain and her story on social media, as one does. Some dug through her feed and noted that she also got the vaccine. You know what happened next—word started circulating that the vaccine killed her baby. (It did not.) She was used as the poster child for the anti-vax movement. Sadly, she had to deal with this absurdity and process the death of her baby at the same time. Conspiracies hurt more people than you may suspect.

Tiffany Dover and Amanda Makulec aren't likely to take legal action. What happens when conspiracy theories and conspiracy theorists go too far? These are just a couple of examples. Let's check out a few others.

Dominion Voting provides many of the voting machines used by US Boards of Election. They provide quality products that do the job well. After the 2020 presidential election, Dominion Voting and its voting machines came under fire. They were accused of being manipulated and rigged. Fox News was a main purveyor of the disinformation surrounding Dominion

Voting. Dominion Voting's reputation suffered as a result. They filed a defamation suit against Fox News Corporation and recently settled for $787.5 million. To prove defamation, one must show that the defendant was negligent and was also aware it was negligent and, essentially, spreading lies.

Several families of the victims of the Sandy Hook School shooting sued Alex Jones, radio show host and conspiracy theorist, for defamation. Jones alleged that the Sandy Hook shooting didn't happen and that it was a staged hoax with actors. The families were getting death threats and faced other obstacles as a result. They pooled their resources and fought back. The families were awarded $1.5 billion.

That is one way to combat conspiracy theories especially if they impact your life. It is difficult if you are fighting the battle alone. There is safety in numbers.

# Let's Talk About It

## Having Conversations About Mis/Disinformation

**I ATTENDED A DINNER RECENTLY** with several women. One of the women mentioned that she had insider information about the United Nations. "The mainstream media aren't covering it," she said. Recall that I said "the media won't cover this" is an indicator that disinformation is afoot. She went on to describe that the UN is sanctioning child marriage and child sexual abuse. She had several links to alternative media outlets that she could share with me if I wanted.

I was gobsmacked. I am writing this book to help everyone navigate the infodemic superhighway and here I was at dinner with not a thing to say. I hadn't heard this particular story, and I was surprised she believed it.

I said that I didn't want those links (though I am curious). I'm afraid of clicking on things like that and then having that stuff follow me around the internet. I then had to weigh whether to have this discussion at a table with about six other people. I decided against it. You need to pick your battles and decide the right time and place. It was clear no one else believed her (we all had that deer in the headlights look about us). I decided to approach her privately at a different time and I did. Did I change her mind? No. But you aren't going to get everyone.

And I can guarantee that if the UN was indeed sanctioning child marriage and child sexual abuse, every mainstream media outlet in the world would be covering it. What are the chances that CNN, the BBC, and other reputable news outlets don't have this info, but Adam in his attic does? Nil.

Invite rather than condemn. I sat down to have the conversation. I did not judge her. I asked questions. I shared my thoughts. We agreed to disagree. Sometimes that's the best you can do. In this chapter, we'll cover how to deal with difficult conversations surrounding disinformation with family, friends, coworkers, and others you encounter daily.

## TALKING TO FAMILY AND FRIENDS

How do you talk to those family members who have gone down the wrong path on the information superhighway? How do you survive holidays and other gatherings like the dinner noted above, when you want to punch your drunk uncle and kick him to the curb? I will still address that, but much of it comes down to . . .

Hate.

There is so much of it.

A recent study by Nathan P. Kalmoe and Lilliana Mason noted that 15 percent of Republicans and 20 percent of Democrats thought we would be better off if members of the other party just died.[26]

Let that sink in.

(Yes, I know what I said about that phrase earlier, but really…let that sink in.)

We want people we disagree with to just die?

I have friends across the political aisle. I don't want them dead, nor do they want me dead (I hope). It's very easy to say and think these things when we don't attach a face to them. Social media allows for a certain degree of anonymity that allows you to wish evil on others because they aren't "real."

How do we get past this? Some argue that the best way to combat hate is to introduce yourself to the "other." Once you sit with someone and talk with them you realize you are not so different. Invite rather than condemn. Think about what it is you want and need. Start with the basics. We all want to have a place to live. We want food and water. We want safety and security. We want to belong and live without fear. We want our children to also have all those things. What we believe and how we get those things may be different, but think about the basics. If it helps, refer to Maslow's Hierarchy of Needs and Herzberg's Motivator Theory.

I had an argument with my brother not too long ago. We are on opposite ends of the political (and health care) spectrum. We were arguing and it was getting heated. It wasn't pretty. Perhaps you relate? He left my house and I felt terrible. So did he. We ended up texting each other that we needed to put a moratorium in place. We would no longer discuss politics or health care when we are together. We said we loved each other and fighting wasn't what we wanted to do when we got together.

So far, so good. There are so many other things to talk about and to share. Turns out we have other things in common that don't require resorting to fisticuffs. Is this something you can do at your celebrations? Also, we noted that we love each other. We do. Can you say the same about those you disagree with? If so, that's a reasonable starting point.

## LONG-TERM STRATEGIES

Let's talk about the larger picture, though. We can get through the holidays and put the kibosh on charged conversations at the dinner table and/or family/friend gatherings. How do we combat the hate that is all around us?

How do we improve our interactions so that we may come into contact with more people who are not like us? Do we have friends or others in our network who are different from us? Can we engage with them and see that they are just like us? What about people who have a different religion? Different race and/or ethnicity? Different gender? Different generation? Instead of trying to find our differences, let's focus on similarities. Let's talk.

More importantly, let's listen and hear.

It helps if you know what you are up against ahead of time. Think about crisis communication. Do we know the warning stage? If we are psyching ourselves up for a holiday dinner, for example, we know the players and we know the buttons that may get pushed—both our own and those of others. Can we prepare for the interaction? You may certainly do what I did with my brother and establish a moratorium on certain topics. That said, we often serve booze at our gatherings and sometimes when enough of it is consumed, all moratoria and bets are off. Prepare for that also.

We could go through a process of social listening to be better prepared for topics that may arise. Do you follow your family on social media? That's often all you need to see and determine what might be top of mind. What topics do they comment on and share? Let's suppose your parents are deep into election-fraud conspiracies. You see them sharing posts online about absentee ballot issues and dead people voting. We can work with that.

What do you do to prepare? And this is a "just in case." With any luck, the topic won't come up, but if it does, you are armed.

What motivates or drives them? What sort of information do they respond to? If you are going to try to convince me of something, you better bring data. In fact, I think my students get frustrated because I will often write, "Based on what data?" when they present a sweeping generalization in a paper they've written. Not everyone wants data. If you are motivated by fear and emotion, that requires a different dynamic. If you don't trust certain sources of information, my quoting those sources to you will just make things worse.

Know your audience. That is key and cannot be stressed enough. In conversations like this, it's not about you, it's about them. Remember we want to invite, not condemn.

If you see something that is suspect, reread it to make sure you've understood what's being conveyed. Then do your own research. Look at the piece. Is just one person quoted? A good journalistic piece will have more than one credible source. Does the piece seem to be biased? If it is a true news piece, it should be as unbiased as possible. If it is an opinion-editorial (op-ed), you should expect a bias. Is the documentation good? If it is a study, was it in a reputable journal? Is nothing taken out of context? Does it seem transparent in content and reporting?

Earlier I mentioned my friend who questioned the validity of the moon landing because of a clip he saw of Buzz Aldrin. Recall what I did. I investigated where that clip came from and saw that it was taken completely out of context. Perhaps you share the entire clip with the person who may have believed otherwise. That won't always work. Recall also what I noted about conspiracy theories. If you present evidence, people then try to dispel the evidence. They may say, "sure, that clip you showed me was fabricated to discredit Buzz. It's not what he really said or did. Artificial Intelligence!" Sometimes you need to let it go for your own sanity.

If you are in a work setting and you need to communicate with the public, you may not have a choice but to try to dispel the myths. Walking away may not be an option. This happened during the pandemic and certainly continues in other areas like politics. Here again, you want to find out why people believe as they do. Did they see a "news" article, or did they follow a particular influencer who may be spewing untruths? Find the source and then do your research. Determine how best to respond. You may need to respond in the media. You may need to reach out to opinion leaders who can share your message. You need to find the trusted source. With any luck, that's you. If not, find that person or group! Monitor what's being said via social listening. Build your plan to respond. Fight the urge to knee jerk in your response. You want to be as thoughtful as possible. You need to ensure you are building trust through authentic and transparent messaging.

If you can control the narrative (prebuttal), you are in pretty good shape. Remember, though, that salacious sells. What you have to say may not be sexy, yet you must counter the prevailing narrative that is. Let's use our furries example. It is much more alarming to say, "Pooping replaced prom as students in high school dressing as cats demand litter boxes," than it is to say, "High schools are not setting up litter boxes."

You do want to be careful that you are truthful in all communication. It would be sassier to say something like, "High school administration shot down request to set up litter boxes so furries have to use the loo like everyone else." That misrepresents because it assumes furries are asking for this concession. Don't feed the beast to attract attention.

I've said that in a work setting you may have no choice but to respond, but that isn't always true. Think about whether you have to. I've had discussions with people about how they can monitor social media comments. You can "censor" comments. If you establish a social media posting policy that outlines what is acceptable and what is not, you can certainly delete posts that violate your policy. For example, you might note that hate speech is not acceptable, so if someone posts a diatribe against a particular group of people that is threatening, you may remove it. No one's rights are violated. They may feel as though they are, but they are incorrect.

I've said it already, but it bears repeating: Refrain from calling anyone "stupid." You may think it until the cows come home but don't say it. In fact, I would urge you not to think it. Remember why people may believe as they do. Most people are not stupid. They are fearful. They are reacting emotionally. They need to belong. They are filling an information void. They suffer personal or historical trauma. Don't discount people because they don't believe as you do or because they don't have your level of knowledge.

# Let's Unpack

## Examples Of Disinformation And Distortions

**YOU'VE READ THE BOOK** and gotten this far. Thank you. Or you just skipped to this step. Bad student, but thank you. I've given several examples of disinformation throughout the book, and they've been primarily from the worlds of health, science, and politics. There are certainly other areas in which we see disinformation. I would like to unpack them here. Keep in mind, these are just the tip of the infodemic iceberg, but I hope they illustrate how you might recognize and dispel disinformation. All examples noted are examples I have seen. I'm not making any of these up!

What I'll do in this chapter is explain in more detail where you may see disinformation. I also want to unpack how I go about determining if something is real or not. What are the steps I take and what is it I look for and find. Please don't look at these examples as the only examples. Sadly, there are many, many, many more.

## SOCIAL MEDIA INFLUENCERS

That's a broad category. Where do I start? Oh, there are so many places and topics. Let me choose fitfluencers or lifestyle influencers. These are people on social media who may have no training and background (authority) at all but espouse often dangerous ideas. Followers trust these people or groups and then follow their advice. Sometimes it doesn't end well.

Many of us are familiar with Gwyneth Paltrow's lifestyle brand, goop. In addition to the website, she also has in-person events. She talks about a number of topics from wellness to family to food. She also sells many products including clothing and candles that smell like her vagina, because "clean cotton" just doesn't cut it. She has been accused on several occasions for espousing dangerous rhetoric related to wellness and health. (To be clear, I am highlighting a couple of instances with examples. I am in no way suggesting that her entire lifestyle line is dangerous. In fact, her website is very clean and nicely organized. I don't get paid enough to buy anything on it, though.)

Several years ago, goop endorsed the use of jade and quartz "eggs" as a method to increase vaginal health. Evidently, women were putting these "eggs" into their vaginas because they were sold as a way to balance hormones and stymie the symptoms of PMS, among other claims. Unfortunately, those claims were shown to be unsubstantiated. goop then noted that it never said there was scientific evidence but rather it was starting a conversation. While that may have been true, one needs to be very careful with what and how something is presented. If people perceive (perceptions—they don't die) this to be a cure for PMS, say, then your "conversation" argument is rather moot.

Medical professionals were up in arms about the claims. The goop site has since removed the claims and paid $145,000 in civil penalties as a result.

If someone who is not a medical professional suggests you buy something to put in any of your nether orifices, please be suspect. Check with an actual medical doctor first.

goop has also been under fire from nutrition professionals for Paltrow's more recent claims about the benefits of bone broth. Again, it was how and what she said. On a podcast she referenced her eating regime by noting she doesn't eat before noon and then eats bone broth. Nutritionists were quick to point out that bone broth can be healthy but not on its own and that a diet so calorie deficient is unhealthy.

If someone is giving nutritional advice, or even seems to, who is not a nutritionist please be suspect. Check with reputable sources. Be careful with how people present information. Paltrow, it seems, thought she was having a conversation with a podcast host. In my viewing of it, I don't think she was giving advice, and she has admitted as much. That said, she is an influencer and whether you like it or not, at a certain level, you are giving advice. People will perceive your responses as advice for them— however incorrect that may be. Your status provides you power and you should wield it responsibly.

Let's not just pick on goop. Other so-called influencers have come under fire for sharing disinformation. If we look at fitfluencers (people who claim to have knowledge of health and fitness), we can see that many are taking advantage of a knowledge of how social media algorithms work and what "sells." Remember salacious? What sells is what's going to "work" to make you bikini-body ready by summer. Generally, fitfluencers look good in a sports bra and leggings that they may have gotten for free to promote on their feeds. It's a vicious, saucy cycle.

And sometimes, the influencer does not endorse the message that is being attributed to them. In another viral TikTok video, former president Barack Obama is seemingly endorsing disinformation. Turns out, a speech he gave at Stanford University was edited to make it seem as though he was speaking in favor of disinformation instead of issuing a warning about disinformation. That video was shared on TikTok and other social media outlets before it was fact-checked and proven to be false. With AI and other technologies, it is very easy to "edit" a video to make it seem as though one thing is being said, when it is very much the opposite. If something seems suspect, please investigate.

## ELECTION DISINFORMATION

If you think disinformation surrounding elections is new, you are incorrect (not stupid). As long as there have been elections, there have been reports of election fraud. Research tells us that while there are incidents of voter fraud, the numbers are so low as to be nonexistent. They certainly aren't enough to sway elections. One study by a political science professor at Brennan Center for Justice at New York University School of Law[27] determined that in all US elections—national down to municipal—between 2000-2014 there were only thirty-one fraudulent ballots.

Yet the perception persists. Historians note that a common method to sell the voter fraud narrative is to use it to prevent certain groups from voting. You may consider gerrymandering in the US as one method to sway elections. Another is to sell a false narrative. In New Jersey[28] in the early 1800s, some women could vote. That didn't sit well with some folks, so they started a disinformation campaign stating that men would vote and then dress up as women to vote again. The solution? Disallow the vote for women—obviously (sarcasm is dripping here).

One of the reasons I became an election-poll worker is so that I had hands-on knowledge of the process and could tell people how elections actually work. I shared that earlier in this book. It would be nearly impossible to "steal" an election in the US. Not so impossible to steal one elsewhere. We see instances of voter fraud or outright election rigging in some countries. Does that help to stoke the fires in this country? Yes. After Donald Trump put forth the idea that the 2020 US election was stolen from him, we saw this same, or a similar narrative pop up in other countries like Peru and Brazil. Sowing the seeds of discontent and dissent.

## BAD DATA

I do want to look at two examples of bad data and bad research, and they are from both sides of the political spectrum in the US. I am always on the lookout for deceptive statistics and research. You can imagine how much fun I am at a party! I've written about trust and context as well as other topics. Let's start with bad data.

I hope everyone followed the case of *Dominion Voting Systems vs. Fox News* I mentioned earlier. If you have not, get on it! It's important!

I was relaxing in my living room, sipping my morning coffee, reading my papers, thinking about which word I would use in Wordle, when I came upon a curious full-page ad from Fox News.

Let's unpack this.

I'm not going to get into why Fox News chose to do this or whether it is, as some have suggested, jury tampering, I want to look at the "data." (As a note, this ad appeared before the settlement with Dominion Voting was reached, hence, the reason I mention jury tampering.) One of the things I try to do is teach people how to recognize misinformation. Then I try to teach people how to communicate about it. Let me walk you through my thought process as I saw this ad:

- An ad for Fox News in *The New York Times*. Interesting choice. Readers of the *Times* would be those who would need to be "convinced" that Fox News is trustworthy. Numerous data sources including those referenced below bear that out.
- TV Networks Most Trusted for News. My first thought here takes me back to the Edelman Trust Barometer. Media aren't necessarily trusted to begin with, and that trust is eroding. We can argue as to why that is, but that's a separate newsletter issue. Hell, that's probably a tome.
- Source: (I didn't even look at the numbers in the ad necessarily because I wanted to know the source of the info. Source and authority are key.) YouGov Profiles. I must admit, I had never heard of YouGov so that gave me pause. Its mission statement from its website says: "Our mission is to supply a continuous stream of accurate data and insight into what the world thinks, so that companies, governments and institutions can make informed decisions." I did some digging on the website and across the web and it seemed legit to me given some of the clients, surveys, and articles written in reputable outlets based on its data. I have since seen other data and research from YouGov, so I feel as though I was closeted. I am familiar with reputable sources, but I do sometimes come across one that I haven't seen. If that's you, take the time to investigate. Remember that disinformationists will use the same tactics as legitimate outlets to try to fool you.

- The brand perception questions noted in the ad: 1. Which of the following do you watch to keep up with the news? (check all) 2. Now that you've listed which TV news networks you watch, which do you most trust for news? (check all). I tried to find this particular survey on the YouGov site, and I couldn't get to those two specific questions. Here is the problem I have with reporting the results this way…I could check that I watch Fox News or CBS or CNN. When asked which I trust, I could safely assume that I trust the outlet I selected. I was unable to find the number of people surveyed or other information related to these specific questions.

What did I find on the website? Well, I did find an *Economist*/YouGov Trust in Media poll from 2022 in which 1,500 adults were surveyed online.[29] I have written about the date of publication and its importance. We might argue that 2022 is not that long ago, but perhaps it is in the news cycle. What were the findings?

- About 30 percent of those who responded said Fox News was trustworthy.
- About 37 percent of those who responded said ABC News, CNN, CBS, and NBC were trustworthy.
- About 27 percent of those who responded said MSNBC was trustworthy.
- The most trusted broadcast outlets were PBS, BBC, and The Weather Channel.

Please note how I phrased the responses. The question was "How trustworthy do you rate the news reported by the following broadcast media organizations?" The responses were on a five-point Likert scale with a "Don't Know" option. The results as I present them above add both "Very Trustworthy" and "Trustworthy" together to get the percentages I reference. It is unclear if that is what the Fox News ad is doing. The first three bullets represent those broadcast media organizations listed in the Fox News ad. PBS, BBC, and The Weather Channel weren't compared because they fared better. That wouldn't make for a compelling ad.

I also found an article referencing the same *Economist*/YouGov poll but with more detailed information.[30] When I was looking at the first poll I referenced, I was unable to drill down to get to how varying demographic audiences feel about each broadcast media organization. For example, it is common knowledge and is backed by facts, that CNN skews liberal and Fox News skews conservative (this poll as well as others note that). It would be expected that those who identify as Republicans would consider Fox News trustworthy and those who identify as Democrats would consider CNN trustworthy (and presumably the other outlet less trustworthy). This article digs into those data. Some key findings:

- The Weather Channel, BBC, and PBS are the most trusted broadcast media organizations overall.
- Democrats most trust PBS, CNN, CBS, NBC the most. They distrust Fox News and Newsmax.
- Republicans most trust Fox News, The Weather Channel, and Newsmax. They distrust nearly all the other organizations.

Again, please note that I was not able to find the 2023 survey information. The above is based on 2022 information. Is it likely to be much different? Could be, but I did find some survey information that noted that not much had changed in trust in broadcast media organizations between 2020 and 2022.

Why do I feel confident with my statements above? I checked the source. I tried to find the survey and absent the specific survey referenced, I found what I believe to be a comparable survey. I checked the methodology. I compared what should be compared to make a statement as noted in the ad "Trusted Now More Than Ever."

My conclusions? If you cherry-pick your findings, you can make anything go your way. Is Fox News trusted? Yes. Is it more trusted than the outlets referenced? Yes, if you drill into the data. Among Republicans, Fox News is more trusted than ABC, CNN, CBS, NBC, and MSNBC. That isn't a surprise. I am bothered that the entire story isn't told. What about PBS, BBC, and The Weather Channel? They come out on top of all broadcast media organizations.

Let's also think about these data and this specific poll. We are relying on public perceptions. Remember that perceptions are real to those who believe them. The poll says nothing about whether we should trust Fox News or any other news outlets. It is based on public opinion.

When you see something that you think might be suspect, investigate. There are many resources out there that are excellent and reputable. One of my favorites—Pew Research—has data from 2021 (again, the date) that notes that, generally speaking, Democrats trust broadcast media more than Republicans. This is backed up by the *Economist*/YouGov data. What Pew Research also notes, is that both parties trust local news organizations while many get news from social media. What is not clear is where/what on social media they use. Anecdotally, I hear people say they get news from social media but it's the news outlets on social media. Okay, that works for me. I would be bothered if it was Drunk Uncle Charlie living on SPAM in his basement who gave you the news (unless he cited a reputable news outlet).

Here are some key takeaways:

- Ask questions.
- Evaluate the source (get as much info as you can).
- Check the date of publication.
- Think strategically—what other info is missing? What other questions do I have?
- Check more than one source.
- Care before you share.

I want to be clear about something. I am not suggesting that Fox News is the only outlet or organization that skews data in its favor. Far from it. As I said, I'm a hit at a party because I love to find these examples.

Also remember, just because I trust something doesn't mean we always should. Due diligence in vetting resources is necessary as I noted above.

I enjoy finding organizations and others using data inappropriately. Here I unpacked what went wrong with this ad and how you can do the same. Caveat: I am not suggesting that this organization is the only company/organization doing this—far from it—but it is a timely example.

## BAD RESEARCH

Now let's look at faulty "research" from the other side of the political spectrum. I follow an account on Instagram that I like very much—@so.informed. It is liberal leaning to be sure. It does break down the day's and week's news into tidbits that are easy to understand, and it presents them in a PowerPoint-like presentation. It is absolutely worth following. I do recommend it.

The owner of the account posted a visual one day with the following verbiage:

"Yesterday, I asked followers from around the world what their thoughts are on the United States. (Resoundingly: we are an international embarrassment.)"

If you go to her Instagram site and find this post, you will see that she posted samples from the responses she received. I do not doubt for a minute that the responses are real. I believe her followers commented as she reported. And I do agree with many of the comments (not that that should be a consideration in determining the quality of "research").

I would expect your followers to believe as you do (confirmation bias). I would expect my followers to believe as I do. Part of what makes social media so fantastic is that we can find others who believe as we do and "hang" with them (echo chamber, filter bubble). That's also what makes social media dangerous.

I would like to stress that I would have to believe she wouldn't call what she did "research" in a scientific sense. So, if I like this account and agree with much of the content, why am I using this post as an example? I can unpack so many things!

Let me get started.

When I give talks about disinformation and misinformation, I include a conversation about why people believe what they believe. Let me start by talking about those as they relate to this social media post and the Fox News "data."

In Chapter 5, I defined confirmation bias, partisan bias, echo chamber, and filter bubble. We see all four of them in action in both cases here.

## Confirmation Bias

I may already hold the beliefs you see on @so.informed. I may not have sought her out, specifically, but when I saw a post and looked at what she had to say, it confirmed my already held beliefs, so I was inclined to follow her. I would argue that confirmation bias might also explain why people follow CNN or Fox News (or other outlets) and may be inclined to believe the data presented about Fox News.

## Partisan Bias

I must believe that she doesn't have many conservatives following her account either here in the US or abroad just by looking at the content she posts. Conversely, I must believe not many liberals are tuned in to Fox News and may question the data presented by Fox News.

## Echo Chamber

I don't need to look elsewhere to get information because I am with others who share my world view. This applies in both cases.

## Filter Bubble

Social media algorithms make it very easy for you to find those who think and feel as you do. There was likely a reason I found @so.informed. I don't know the person behind the account (or I don't think I do). I must have liked others who follow her, or I must have liked similar content for her account to show up in my social media feed. The same would apply to Fox News. I may not know anyone working there but perhaps I found the news outlet via social media.

What does this mean in the context of the issues at hand? I will use myself as an example.

I hold certain beliefs. I tend to look for others who feel as I do. Why? I want to hang out with like-minded individuals. That doesn't mean I don't hang out with others. I certainly do, but the bulk of my friends share my views. Why don't I seek out those who don't share my views? Have you ever attended a party and talked to that person who you find doesn't share your views? It was likely not comfortable. Of course, we should get out of our comfort zones from time to time but doing so causes stress. Don't we already have enough stress in our lives?

I could say that all my friends believe just as those who responded to this social media post on @so.informed. The way the responses are presented in her post might lead you to believe that everyone in the world shares this viewpoint. We all know that isn't true. Could it be a majority viewpoint? It could, but we won't know that without quality research.

And what would that look like?

You would need to ask the question of those beyond your followers. You would need to do some random sampling of a representative group of people. This was neither. (Again, I want to stress that I have a feeling she wasn't going for a scientific research study.)

What does random sampling mean? You would choose a representative sample from a population of people. To truly do this justice would require much time and money.

Seeing this post reminded me of some of the narratives I'd heard after our last presidential election. I remember a journalist interviewing people who voted for Donald Trump. The interviewee said he believed the election was stolen because everyone he knew in his neighborhood voted for Trump. How could the other person have won?

Confirmation bias.

I am sure there are those who could say just the opposite. "All the people in my neighborhood voted for Joe Biden so that's why he won." We do tend to get an inflated view of the truth because of our biases.

The moral to this story? Be careful what you post, because I'm coming for you! Also, be wary when you see ads or social media posts that seem to be missing something or misrepresenting something. It's okay to ask questions and to dig deeper.

Always care before you share.

## SCIENCE VS. FAITH

National Pride Month has become quite a hot-button issue. It's a month in which we celebrate our similarities rather than our differences and encourage unity with our LGBTQ+ community, recognizing their contributions, culture, and achievements. Also in June is the United Nations International Day for Countering Hate Speech. Coincidence?

One of the arguments I often hear against those who identify as LGBTQ+ is that this behavior is so unnatural and against what God has decreed (men and women should be together to procreate—it's God's will). Or, if you don't believe in God, we need to procreate because it's natural to continue the species.

I'm here to challenge those narratives.

Let's go back in time a bit. I was fortunate to attend the summer program at the Duke University Marine Laboratory in 1990. I took two classes: marine ecology and physiology of marine invertebrates. I know what you're thinking: Pauline, you sure know how to summer.

One of our field trips included an encounter with dolphins. One of the cetacean (fauna order that includes dolphins and whales) researchers took my class out on one of the boats to study a pod of dolphins (essentially a herd of dolphins). To say that this was amazing is an understatement, but you're probably wondering what this has to do with Pride Month.

We saw two of the dolphins engaging in behavior that looked sexual and being college students, we commented and giggled and maybe said something about animal porn. I believe a student even asked how to tell the sex of the dolphins apart and to help us to identify which was female and which was male.

The researcher's response? They are both male. Then she went on to explain to us that many animals exhibit behavior that we would consider homosexual. It blew my 20-year-old mind. What? Homosexual behavior in the animal kingdom? That's fantastic! How are we not hearing about this?

I think we know why we are not hearing about this. I don't need to explain. But I will.

Bias. Negative attitudes. Politics. Religion. Ignorance. Faith vs. science.

Scientists have seen same sex behavior in several animals including invertebrates, but I want to focus on mammals. Why? Because we are mammals. We are not so far removed from other mammals. It's nature... and perfectly natural.

It does present as a Darwinian Paradox. Are you familiar with Charles Darwin (I own his book *On the Origin of Species* because, of course I do)? He proposed the Theory of Evolution based on the idea of natural selection. We are all descended from a common ancestor, and we have all evolved through the process of natural selection. What does that mean?

Billions of years ago, life on Earth formed. Organisms that we know today evolved from a single-celled creature and formed life as we know it...over years and years and years. Creatures evolved and adapted to their surroundings.

Darwin's Paradox describes behavior that seems to contradict natural selection—same sex behavior, for example. If we are here to procreate and carry on the species, same sex behavior seems counterintuitive (the paradox to natural selection). Same sex behavior does not seem to impart any obvious reproductive benefit. Same sex partners cannot reproduce by themselves.

Pause for a moment.

Are you thinking that I am proving the point of homophobes everywhere?

Ah, but wait.

A blog post on the National Wildlife Federation website explains very well that the Paradox may not be quite so paradoxical.[31] Same-sex behavior is incredibly common in the animal kingdom. Scientists have identified more than 1,500 animals that exhibit same-sex behaviors. Why? Recent research suggests we should ask, "Why not?" instead.

Scientists have posited that while evolution favors reproductive advantages, it may also favor non-reproductive advantages. (As a woman who is child-free by choice, this appeals to me and makes so much sense.) Research suggests that same-sex relationships and behaviors do serve a purpose. Perhaps reproduction isn't the only thing we should focus on. Same-sex relationships provide a benefit that is different from, but just as important as, reproduction. Some of those benefits may include stress reduction and community building. It is also argued that heterosexual behavior evolved from homosexual behavior. What?

Think about it. "In order for an animal to choose one sex over the other, they must first be able to determine the difference between a male or female of the same species. And for these sex-specific differences to evolve, sexual reproduction must evolve from asexual reproduction (cloning) first. Therefore, there must have been some time after sexual reproduction evolved and before sexual signaling evolved, where animals had no choice but to mate indiscriminately."

Sounds like a Saturday night in my twenties.

We approach survival based on costs and benefits. Very economical. Recent research also posits that we may be approaching this the wrong way. *Scientific American* addressed recent studies on the subject.[32]

We assume that same-sex relationships are costly in that they don't produce offspring to carry on the species. How many heterosexual relationships don't produce offspring? (Ahem.) How long does it take couples, sometimes, to produce offspring? Isn't that costly?

Let's also consider that nature is quite good at establishing its equilibrium. Every creature does not need to reproduce! Look at humans. Do we all need to be procreating? The world cannot sustain that (we humans don't seem to have our own natural checks and balances).

Asking "why not" instead of "why" is an interesting approach.

And while we are at it, think about hate and hate speech. Why do we hate? Why not stop? Same-sex behaviors are perfectly natural, and we should be accepting of behaviors and attitudes that are different from our own without having to ridicule, accuse, point fingers, or hate.

Accepting that we all have a purpose and that those purposes aren't necessarily at cross-purposes is key. (I need a thesaurus.)

Science bumped up against faith. The winner is…

## PUBLIC HEALTH VICTORIES THAT WERE ANYTHING BUT

Many of us may not understand what public health is and what it has done. Public health is concerned with the health of the public. It does encompass what you may normally think of as health care like disease prevention, but it also includes things like motor vehicle safety.

One of the most significant achievements of public health over the last 100 years is motor vehicle safety, which includes legislation mandating seat belt use.

How was this initially received by the public? You can probably guess. "You are taking away my right to choose for myself." "You are invading my privacy." Does this sound familiar? Initially you are going to have pushback on initiatives. Now? How many people do you know who complain about having to wear a seatbelt? Not many. You might argue that I am living in an echo chamber and perhaps there are people complaining, but when you take a look at the data, it's difficult to dispute that public health does look out for population health even if it's not popular at the time of implementation.

The CDC notes that those who wear seat belts have their risk of death reduced by 45 percent and the risk of serious injury by 50 percent.[33] Those are some nice numbers.

Why do I raise this issue because it doesn't seem like disinformation. It isn't based on my definition of disinformation. I do bring it up because before many initiatives become recommendations or laws, they go through this period of scrutiny that may lead to disinformation and conspiracies.

Recall that I mentioned fluorinated water earlier. Before cities and towns started adding fluoride to water (another public health success), there were protests. Some of the messaging stated that fluoride rots your teeth, which is the opposite of what it actually does. Some of the people sounding this alarm were nurses. That gave many people pause because they are medical people who should know. But are they the "right" medical people? Much research existed noting that fluoride helps keep our teeth strong.

Think also about what must have been in place for municipalities to add fluoride to drinking water. Science and politics working together. How long does it take initiatives to take hold in your towns and cities? So, if something like this were to take place there must be much scientific consensus. Likely one of the selling points was that adding fluoride would cut medical costs significantly. Cost cutting usually sells.

## FURRIES

We've already talked a bit about this nutty concept, but I have to go here again because it's one of those conspiracies that has nine lives and just won't die.

When I first heard about the idea of school children identifying as cats and demanding litter boxes in school, I laughed out loud. I thought someone was quoting a satirical article to me. I didn't give it much thought until I started seeing politicians and others using it as political fodder. I had to investigate. What did I do?

My first instinct was to Google: "Are furries demanding litter boxes in schools?" I saw several articles referencing this alleged phenomenon. Then I Googled: "Evolution of furries conspiracy theory." At this point I realized that's what this was.

Let's back up a second. What are furries, and are they real? There are people who dress up as animals. They do this for fun and don't necessarily "identify" as animals as one might identify as male or female.

What did I find in my search? Bruce Bostelman, a senator from Nebraska, publicly proclaimed that furries were disrupting classrooms with purring and hissing and they needed litter boxes. Other commentators jumped on the bandwagon and reiterated that they had heard the same thing.

Why did I care? I've mentioned that when I was working at our local polling place, someone said to me that our local high school had to install litter boxes. I said that this was just a myth and not true. This person insisted, so I reached out to the president of our school board who is a very good friend. She confirmed what I already knew, which was that there were no litter boxes in schools, and no one was dressing as cats or other animals unless it was Halloween, and then it was a sexy cat. I was still not believed.

Let that sink in.

I took my investigation a few steps further. I asked my colleagues who teach in our journalism program if this were occurring, would the media cover it (remember that "the media won't cover it" is a common refrain among disinformationists). They said if schools had litter boxes, the media would be all over. Media often cover school board meetings, and this would be discussed at school board meetings.

Hmmm. Would it? I asked a couple of other school administrators if something like this would be addressed at school board meetings. They said yes. I also asked these administrators if litter boxes were allowed anywhere. They all said it was completely untrue, but it was a story that kept rearing its ugly head from time to time. One even noted that the custodial staff said they would quit if they had to start cleaning litter boxes.

Then I thought that the local health department might need to be notified as this might constitute something that would be regulated by the health department. I didn't poll all health departments in the US, but I did ask my local health department. It was confirmed that this was a hoax and that the state health department would likely need to be involved.

I would also offer this. While many schools do not allow students to use their cell phones in class, this generation of students is rarely without them and tends to document everything including what they eat. If there were litter boxes in schools, I would have to believe that we would see photos on Instagram and other places. I have yet to see any.

I don't expect everyone to go through the steps I outlined above, but that might be what it takes. I can present evidence from what I consider reliable sources—if litter boxes needed to be installed, certainly the president of the school board would know about it. I imagine the board would need to approve such a request.

If our local school was installing litter boxes, you can be sure a reputable news source would cover it. My journalism colleagues would be finding a student who identified as a cat and interviewing that feline. They would then seek out comment from teachers, environmental services staff who would have to empty the litter boxes, and from the superintendent and school board. This story would be plenty salacious!

Yet all you hear are stories. Don't believe the hype.


## WHAT'S NEXT?

Allow me to predict the future.

By the time you read this, I can guarantee the infodemic will still be raging. I can assure you that disinformationists will still be creating and people will still be believing.

We will still question what is true and what is not.

We will question new technologies and, perhaps, consider them a fad.

We will harbor a healthy skepticism toward information that we see online whether on social media or unfamiliar websites.

One thing I hope we all do—care before you share. Ask questions. Seek knowledge. Look for the truth.

# Where Do We Go From Here?

**WE *SHOULD* BAN** accounts on social media that create and spread disinformation. We *should* establish fines or other punishments for those who create and spread disinformation. We are in big trouble because disinformation is just going to get worse with artificial intelligence. We must act, but what should we do?

We should worry about disinformation, because its proliferation spells the end of democracy as we know it. It is a problem when people believe things that aren't true that will have a negative effect on their lives. We should also worry when we talk about stifling free speech in any way. It is the hallmark of a healthy democracy.

We have the tools we need to inoculate ourselves. We just need to use them. Education. Trust. Transparency. Communication. Truth.

That sounds Pollyannaish, doesn't it?

If we just educate people, they will be smarter. Yes, and perhaps we can also teach them to think critically.

If we trust others or trust the right people, the world will be a better place. Yes, and establishing trust is a long, arduous, sometimes tortuous process.

If we let them see behind the Wizard's curtain, all will be well. Yes, and showing your true nature will lead people to trust . . . or not.

If we communicate, people will have the right messages and know what to do. Yes, and we bolster interactions that may lead to increased trust.

If we tell the truth the world will right itself. Yes, and we can all sleep soundly at night.

That sounds easy. But it also sounds like the rhetoric we hear from disinformationists. Recall that I said the people creating disinformation are doing all the right things, minus the evil and lying. They know who their audience is. They know their pain points. They know what motivates them. They know how to reach them. They appear to be trustworthy and transparent. They communicate well. They tell the truth—or at least their version of it.

We need to do the same. Know our audience. Know their pain points. Know what motivates them. Know how to reach them. Be trustworthy and transparent. Above all else, tell the truth.

The pushback you will get is obvious. *Why should I trust you? How do I know you are telling the truth? "They" (whom I trust) said you would say this!*

This requires work. The answer isn't something we can find in a day or week or even a year. So much of what we are seeing is a result of years and years of distrust. There has been a slow chiseling away at the bedrock of many of our institutions including education, government, science, health, and education by disinformationists. To a certain degree, we allowed this to happen without addressing the problem. Did we think it was a fad? That it would go away? That people would embrace reason?

We now have people who are living in what some psychologists suggest is an "alternate reality." They don't realize that the information that is fed to them is designed to keep them in this bubble. It will be difficult for us to penetrate it and reach them.

The solution is far from easy. What I outlined above is what I think we need to do. That said, you must do the work. That means "boots on the ground" work like getting out into the community and being the truth, admitting errors, and reaching people where they are. To do this, use your ethos and pathos skills at the same time. In some circles, I am Dr. Pauline Hoffmann. In others, I am Pauline. Can you do the same? Can you be authentic and trustworthy and relatable? Can you build authentic trust?

It may also help to learn some tips and tricks from disinformationists. I challenge you to a disinformation campaign-creating game. It is very easy to create and disseminate disinformation. Several tools exist that allow you to play a game while also educating. I encourage you to look at each game noted below and share!

- **Go Viral** is a quick game that you may play that will help you better understand some of the tactics used in disseminating Covid-19-specific disinformation.
  **www.goviralgame.com**

- **Cranky Uncle** is similar to Go Viral in that it helps you—or rather your cranky uncle helps you—determine what is true and what is not. It helps you to recognize the fallacies often used in creating disinformation.
  **app.crankyuncle.info/language**

- **Bad News** allows you to create "fake news" using many of the same tactics used by disinformationists. You can keep score to see how you compare with others. Are you better at creating disinformation than your friend?
  **www.getbadnews.com**

- **Fake It to Make It** allows you to "create" a fake news site that you may monetize (not really). It highlights how easy it is to create fake news and how people do it to make money because you can.
  **www.fakeittomakeitgame.com**

## WHAT IS BEING DONE?

So many organizations worldwide are tackling disinformation. The information I am about to share is current as of this writing. Please note that it may change. For the most complete list, please visit my website at datadoyenne.com. If you know of an organization or individual not included, please reach out. I want to make sure work in this area is recognized.

There is hope on several fronts. Many people and organizations are tackling the infodemic. Much information exists to help navigate this tortured road.

Some sites and organizations doing good work include:

- WHO MythBusters
- News Literacy Project
- Society for Infodemic Management
- Misinfo Rx
- American Association for the Advancement of Science
- The Media Manipulation Casebook
- AFP-Fact Check (Agence France-Presse)
- PolitiFact
- AllSides
- Birds Aren't Real
- Mafindo (Indonesian Anti-defamation Society)
- Alt News in India (founders Mohammed Zubair and Prati K Sinha)
- International Fund for Public Interest Media
- Institute for Global Policy (Columbia University)
- Project Ages
- Global Coalition for Journalism (#HoldTheLine)
- #RelaimOurRights
- International Panel on the Information Environment
- Mercury Project (Georgetown Institute)
- Orato
- Election Integrity Partnership
- Disinformation Defense League
- Countering Truth Decay (RAND)
- #FactsFirst

## COUNTRIES TAKE ACTION

Many countries have acted against disinformation in a number of arenas from health and science to politics. The Media Literacy Index is created by the Open Society Institute in Sofia, Bulgaria.[34] It measures how well countries can identify misinformation. The index is determined based on press freedom, education and trust in people. The top five European countries are Finland, Norway, Denmark, Estonia, and Sweden.

Finland has been number one for two years running. It has incorporated media literacy into its curriculum starting in preschool. Elements are taught in all fields from math to physical education. Students are taught how to identify misinformation in several outlets including the news and social media. Finland does have one of the best education systems in the world, we may still learn from them.

Other countries are using media literacy but are also taking different actions.[35] Some countries like Canada, Mexico, Sweden, and Spain have established task forces. The US, Chile, Brazil, and Russia have developed bills to combat disinformation. China, France, and Belarus have established laws against disinformation. As disinformation becomes more prevalent, other actions are likely to be taken.

This will certainly be an area to watch.

## JOURNALISM

I've mentioned that journalism is a key in fighting disinformation. We need to ensure we have a free press but that doesn't exist worldwide. Even in the US, news outlets are cutting back or shuttering altogether. That leaves a news desert in many areas, particularly rural areas. Additionally, one newspaper or one news outlet towns are dangerous because competition does breed excellence in many ways. Many countries prevent unbiased news from reaching its citizens by putting up "walls" to prevent people from accessing information. Think China and Russia, to name just two. Think also about the danger foreign correspondents face. As of this writing, *Wall Street Journal* reporter, Evan Gershkovich, is being held in a Russian prison on charges of espionage. The US has declared him to be wrongfully detained.

The News Literacy Project is active in the US in helping teachers and others deal with disinformation. It provides much education that may be used at several different grade levels and partners with journalists to help deliver information. They have regular fact checking and share that information via newsletter and online.

## LITERACY EDUCATION AND COMMUNICATION

One thing most infodemiologists agree on is the need for literacy education. Literacy is important at every grade level, but it needs to start with young kids.

It should surprise no one that an educator is recommending education. United Nations Secretary-General António Guterres writes of education:

*"It's the bedrock of societies, economies, and every person's potential.
But without adequate investment, this potential will wither on the vine.
It has always been shocking to me that education has been given
such a low priority in many government policies and in international
cooperation instruments.
The theme of this year's International Day of Education reminds us
that "to invest in people, prioritize education."*

Invest in people, prioritize education. ***Amen!***

# Acknowledgements

**THE DANGER** in writing acknowledgments is that someone is inadvertently left off the list. I agonize over omission! To prevent undue anxiety, I won't mention any specific person by name. You know who you are and if you think you are that person, sure. I'll go with that.

First and foremost, thank you to all those working on the infodemic. You are the unsung heroes. Your work is often thankless, time consuming, frustrating, and dangerous. The fight is worth it. Keep it up.

Thank you to scientists, educators, and public health practitioners. The contributions you've made to educating us and keeping us healthy and safe cannot be praised enough. You also work in dangerous times.

To communicators who are charged with distilling complex ideas and sharing them with the masses, good luck but don't quit.

Thank you to the World Health Organization Infodemic Manager Training Program. You came along in my life at just the right time. The information I got and contacts I made are invaluable. They form the basis of this book. While I have long studied and been fascinated by conflict, the training program took it to the next level and set me on this path. You've created a monster.

Thank you to numerous colleagues and friends who had to listen to me talk about conspiracies and fake news and witch hunts and this book for ages. Bad news: It won't stop.

To Broad Book Press for taking a chance on me. I hope this is the start of a long and fruitful relationship.

To my brother and my husband who both said they won't read this book because they aren't readers, I will offer the audio book when it's available. To my sister who will read this because I told her she must.

Both have always been incredibly supportive of me and have also mocked my nerdiness. Thank you to my mom for her sense of humor and candor. Thank you to my niece who will inherit my estate. It stands at about $10.27. Get ready!

Finally, to my dad. You always taught me to stand up for what is right and to fight for my beliefs. I am reminded that you said if we have a skill or knowledge that others need and don't have, it behooves us to share it. You also had no idea where my interest in science and communication came from, but you certainly nurtured it. I toast your spirit.

# About The Author

Meet **DR. PAULINE W. HOFFMANN**, affectionately known as the Data Doyenne, a title she wears with pride and a hint of playful curiosity. Born and raised on a serene 40-acre land east of Buffalo, New York, Pauline's childhood was a blend of outdoor adventures and a deep-seated fascination with the pages of *National Geographic*—sharks, in particular, captured her imagination and sparked a lifelong passion for understanding the misunderstood.

Her journey from a science-enthused youngster charting utility bills for fun to a Ph.D. holder is as unconventional as it is inspiring. After a stint at St. Bonaventure University, where dreams of studying biology clashed humorously with its landlocked locale, Pauline's path took a pivotal turn following her father's death. This led her into the realms of public relations and creative services within healthcare, where she discovered a love for leadership, strategy, and the power of data in storytelling.

Pauline's academic pursuits didn't stop there; she dove back into education, earning master's and doctoral degrees focused on communication in conflict. Today, she stands as a revered professor, teaching almost exclusively online and continuously refining the art of virtual education.

But it's not all academia for Pauline. The onset of the Covid-19 pandemic propelled her to launch Data Doyenne, aiming to counteract the infodemic with a dose of science and reason. Her mission? To make data literacy accessible and engaging, turning the data nervous into data nerds.

Beyond her professional endeavors, Pauline's life is rich with personal passions. Alongside her husband, she tends to a bustling farm, raising chickens, ducks, bees, and dogs. She also runs an all-natural body care company, marrying her scientific expertise with her creative flair. Her interests in tarot reading and travel underscore her commitment to exploring and sharing diverse cultures and perspectives.

Pauline invites you on a captivating data journey, blending her unique blend of expertise, humor, and real-world experiences to demystify the complex web of fake news, witch hunts, and conspiracy theories. Join her as she navigates the truth through the lens of an infodemiologist, ensuring the ride is anything but dull.

# Bibliography

1.  McCorkindale, T., & Henry, A. (2022, February 22). 2022 *IPR disinformation in society report*. Institute for Public Relations. https://instituteforpr. org/2022-disinformation-report/

2.  Edelman. (2023). 2023 *Edelman Trust Barometer*. Edelman. https://www. edelman.com/trust/2023/trust-barometer

3.  Borges do Nascimento, I. J., Beatriz Pizarro, A., Almeida, J., Azzopardi-Muscat, N., André Gonçalves, M., Björklund, M., & Novillo-Ortiz, D. (2022). Infodemics and health misinformation: a systematic review of reviews. *Bulletin of the World Health Organization*, 100(9), 544–561. https://doi.org/10.2471/blt.21.287654

4.  French, J., & Raven, B. (1959, January). *The bases of social power*. ResearchGate. https://www.researchgate.net/ publication/215915730_The_bases_of_social_power

5.  Swint, K. C. (2008). *Mudslingers : the twenty-five dirtiest political campaigns of all time : countdown from no. 25 to no. 1*. Union Square Press.

6.  Watling, E. (2019, March 13). *The 200-Year History of the Anti-Vaxxer Movement: From "Cowpox Face" to Autism Claims*. Newsweek; Newsweek. https://www. newsweek.com/history-anti-vaxxers-vaccination-1358403

7.  REPORTER, C. S. N. S. (2023, January 17). *Buffalo has stopped adding fluoride to water system for the last 7 years*. Buffalo News. https://buffalonews.com/ buffalo-has-stopped-adding-fluoride-to-water-system-for-the-last-7-years/ article_b729ffeb-b46e-55b5-aaed-c98f6691d0bc.html

8.  Gounder, C. (2023, January 28). Grant Wahl Was a Loving Husband. I Will Always Protect His Legacy. *The New York Times*. https://www.nytimes. com/2023/01/08/opinion/grant-wahl-celine-gounder-vaccine.html

9.  Vigen, T. (n.d.). Spurious Correlations. Tylervigen.com. https://tylervigen. com/spurious-correlations

10. Division, I. S. (n.d.). *Library Guides: Evaluating Resources: Home*. Guides.lib. berkeley.edu. Retrieved March 1, 2024, from https://guides.lib.berkeley. edu/evaluating-resources#:~:text=When%20you%20encounter%20any%20 kind%20of%20source%2C%20consider%3A

11. Collier, R. (2016). Dairy research: "Real" science or marketing?. *Canadian Medical Association Journal*, 188(10), 715–716. https://doi.org/10.1503/ cmaj.109-5278

12. *The Disinformation Dozen*. (2021, March 24). Center for Countering Digital Hate | CCDH. https://counterhate.com/research/the-disinformation-dozen/

13. *How to Spot Disinformation | Union of Concerned Scientists*. (n.d.). Www.ucsusa. org. https://www.ucsusa.org/resources/how-spot-disinformation

14. Mitchell, A., Jurkowitz, M., Oliphant, J. B., & Shearer, E. (2020, July 30). *Americans Who Mainly Get Their News on Social Media Are Less Engaged, Less Knowledgeable*. Pew Research Center's Journalism Project; Pew Research Center. https://www.pewresearch.org/journalism/2020/07/30/ americans-who-mainly-get-their-news-on-social-media-are-less-engaged- less-knowledgeable/

15. Institute, J. (2022, July 27). *What data can tell us about the state of health in Cattaraugus County*. Jandoli Institute. https://jandoli.net/2022/07/27/ what-data-can-tell-us-about-the-state-of-health-in-cattaraugus-county/

16. Nyhan, B., Settle, J. E., Thorson, E., Wojcieszak, M., Barberá, P., Chen, A. Y., Allcott, H., Brown, T., Crespo-Tenorio, A., Dimmery, D., Freelon, D., Gentzkow, M., González-Bailón, S., Guess, A. M., Kennedy, E. H., Young Mie Kim, Lazer, D., Malhotra, N., Moehler, D. C., & Pan, J. (2023). Like-minded sources on Facebook are prevalent but not polarizing. *Nature*, 620(7972), 137–144. https://doi.org/10.1038/s41586-023-06297-w

17. Pace, K. (2016). *Trust is one of the most important aspects of relationships*. MSU Extension. https://www.canr.msu.edu/news/ trust_is_one_of_the_most_important_aspects_of_relationships

18. Brown, B. (2021). *Dare to Lead The BRAVING Inventory*. Brené Brown. https:// brenebrown.com/resources/the-braving-inventory/

19. Gramlich, J. (n.d.). *Young Americans are less trusting of other people – and key institutions – than their elders*. Pew Research Center. Retrieved March 1, 2024, from https://www.pewresearch.org/short-reads/2019/08/06/ young-americans-are-less-trusting-of-other-people-and-key-institutions- than-their-elders/#:~:text=Americans%20believe%20trust%20has%20 declined%20in%20their%20country%2C

20. Ortiz-Ospina, E., & Roser, M. (2016). *Trust*. Our World in Data. https://ourworldindata.org/trust

21. Iacucci, A. A. (2017, March 6). *Stop saying you want to give voice to the voiceless!* The Unwilling Colonizer. https://anahiayala.com/2017/03/06/stop-saying-you-want-to-give-voice-to-the-voiceless/

22. Haugen, J. (2022, May 9). *The Problem with "Giving a Voice to the Voiceless."* Rooted. https://rootedstorytelling.com/rethinking-tourism/voice-for-the-voiceless-dominant-culture/

23. *The Conspiracy Chart* 2021. (n.d.). Conspiracychart.com. https://conspiracychart.com/

24. Krugman, P. (2023, February 28). Opinion | Conspiracy Theorizing Goes Off the Rails. *The New York Times*. https://www.nytimes.com/2023/02/27/opinion/east-palestine-train-derailment-conspiracy-theories.html

25. Makulec, A. (2022, May 11). Opinion | I Lost My Baby. Then Antivaxxers Made My Pain Go Viral. *The New York Times*. https://www.nytimes.com/2022/05/11/opinion/vaccines-antivaxxers-pregnancy.html

26. Kalmoe, N., & Mason, L. (2019). *Lethal Mass Partisanship: Prevalence, Correlates, & Electoral Contingencies*. https://www.dannyhayes.org/uploads/6/9/8/5/69858539/kalmoe___mason_ncapsa_2019_-_lethal_partisanship_-_final_lmedit.pdf

27. *What Research Tells Us About Voter Fraud.* (n.d.). Evidencebasedliving. human.cornell.edu. https://evidencebasedliving.human.cornell.edu/blog/what-research-tells-us-about-voter-fraud/

28. *What Research Tells Us About Voter Fraud.* (n.d.). Evidencebasedliving. human.cornell.edu. https://evidencebasedliving.human.cornell.edu/blog/what-research-tells-us-about-voter-fraud/

29. *Economist/YouGov Poll: March 26-29, 2022 — Trust in Media | YouGov.* (n.d.). Today.yougov.com. Retrieved March 1, 2024, from https://today.yougov.com/politics/articles/41960-economistyougov-poll-march-26-29-2022-trust-media?redirect_from=%2Ftopics%2Fpolitics%2Farticles-reports%2F2022%2F04%2F05%2Feconomistyougov-poll-march-26-29-2022-trust-media

30. *Trust in Media 2022: Where Americans get their news and who they trust for information | YouGov.* (n.d.). Today.yougov.com. https://today.yougov.com/politics/articles/41957-trust-media-2022-where-americans-get-news-poll?redirect_from=%2Ftopics%2Fpolitics%2Farticles-reports%2F2022%2F04%2F05%2Ftrust-media-2022-where-americans-get-news-poll

31. Hardt, B. (2022, June 6). *New Science on Same-sex Behavior in Wildlife • The National Wildlife Federation Blog.* The National Wildlife Federation Blog. https://blog.nwf.org/2022/06/new-science-on-same-sex-behavior-in-wildlife/

32. McDonough, A. K. M. G. L. (2019, November 20). *Why Is Same-Sex Sexual Behavior So Common in Animals?* Scientific American Blog Network. https://blogs.scientificamerican.com/observations/why-is-same-sex-sexual-behavior-so-common-in-animals/

33. CDC. (2020, November 3). *Policy Impact: Seat Belts | Motor Vehicle Safety | CDC Injury Center.* Www.cdc.gov. https://www.cdc.gov/transportationsafety/seatbeltbrief/index.html

34. *How It Started, How It is Going: Media Literacy Index 2022.* (n.d.). Osis.bg. https://osis.bg/?p=4243&lang=en

35. Funke, D., & Flamini, D. (2018). *A guide to anti-misinformation actions around the world - Poynter.* Poynter. https://www.poynter.org/ifcn/anti-misinformation-actions/